## Praise for *BECOMI*

"Dr. Broadhead has tapped into the collective spirit of educators: we doubt, we strive, we hope, we dig, we believe. His journey is all of our journeys with a much needed introspection on the mission to being an effective teacher and making a difference. *Becoming Enough* is a poignant tale that many of us educators know all too well. Dr. Broadhead has taken the educator's vulnerabilities and weaved them into a story full of painful lessons, hopeful beliefs, and an unrelenting work ethic. This book reminded me why I continue to teach."

–Dr. Brian Harmon, ELA, Teacher

"The field of education has been in crisis for at least 30 years. No community has suffered more from this crisis than students of color and communities of poverty. *Becoming Enough* is an engaging reflection from a passionate educator navigating his way through a system that can at times be corrupt and difficult, and finding his path to influence and excellence. In an era where Black male educators are leaving the field of education, I hope that this book inspires the reader to take the challenge that Dr. Broadhead accepted, and consider the field of education as a pathway to become a positive agent for change in communities of need."

–Anthony Muhammad, PhD, Educational Consultant and Bestselling Author

"With equal parts reflection, humility, pride, and transparency, Marcus Broadhead has provided us with lighthouses for servant leaders to shape their core values, while shaping school culture.

Through this window into his leadership soul, every established and aspiring leader has a safe place to examine their own soul. His style and stories are so real and relatable, that before you realize it, you're refining, reinforcing, and even reimagining how you lead from where you are."

–Ken Williams, Author, Speaker, Disruptor, Unfold the Soul

"Dr. Marcus Broadhead does an amazing job of walking you through his journey as a young black male navigating the public education landscape. His story is powerful, and the lessons he learned along the way will help every educator grow in their profession.

*Becoming Enough* will capture your heart and mind, and it will challenge your thinking about issues you may not even be aware exist in public education. I am a school principal with over 10 years of experience in school leadership, and I found myself reflecting on how I address different situations in my own school. How do I create an environment that helps me recruit and retain amazing young educators, and what could I do better in order to help them develop into strong future school leaders?

If you want a book that will challenge your thinking, open your eyes to the world of education from a unique perspective, and help you grow as an educator then I highly recommend that you pick this book up!"

–Robert F. Breyer, Principal, Author, Speaker

# BECOMING ENOUGH

# BECOMING ENOUGH

## AN EDUCATOR'S JOURNEY TO LEADERSHIP

DR. MARCUS L. BROADHEAD

Aid & Tailored
LEADERSHIP CONSULTING
PRESS, LLC

Some names and identifying details have been changed to protect the privacy of individuals.

Aid & Tailored
LEADERSHIP CONSULTING
PRESS, LLC

To contact the author about booking talks, workshops, or bulk orders of this book, visit www.marcusbroadhead.com

Editor: David Hogan
Book Design: Christy Day, Constellationbookservices.com

ISBN (paperback): 979-8-9856431-0-7
ISBN (ebook): 979-8-9856431-1-4

Library of Congress Control Number: 2022930898

Printed in the United States of America

# A BRIEF NOTE

My experiences as an educator come with a clarity now that did not exist during my journey. Everything I share is in the spirit of reflection. I recognize two things: who I was, I needed to be at that time. Secondly, I speak for myself. Although I represent a gender, an ethnicity and a specific region, my experiences are unique to me. The essence of the challenges I have faced is predicated upon the notion that I speak and act for everyone who looks like me. Although I may be a pretty damn good representative, all that makes me who I am is my collective understanding. My fears, challenges and passion most certainly can be shared and understood by Black men, but I do not carry the expectation that all Black men will identify with what I have chosen to share. This educator's experiences reflect a greater understanding for the work that is needed, and how all educators can pull from my mistakes without making the same ones. It is my sole purpose and life's work to help, educate and inspire.

# CONTENTS

# ACKNOWLEDGMENTS

This book is the manifestation not just of my life experiences but of the patience and support from those who love me and have believed in my gifts before I believed in myself. Most specifically I would like to thank my wife Lisa for telling me with every breath to "just pick one of those books and finish something." I would like to thank Andre Samuels who, through his leadership coaching, helped me to "stand in my confidence." Lastly, I would like to acknowledge Marguerite Golden Rhodes for being an exemplar of a leader. As my elementary school principal she showed me what it meant to make a difference in the lives of children. God bless her soul.

# PART ONE

# TEACHING KINDA SORT OF

# MR. B vs. MARCUS BROADHEAD

The panel sat across from me and I, nervously smiling, stared back while trying to determine what any one of them was thinking before being interrupted by the question, "Why do you want to be a teacher?" I paused before responding, as rehearsed. My friends told me that this was a good interview technique.

> Friends [in magnanimous sincerity]: "You have to pause. Don't rush to respond. Even if you know the answer, just give it a minute."

None of them were in education. They were older than I and had recently been hired in their respective fields, which made them experts. I chalked this up to experience so I listened.

The question lingered and I, having thought about this before, ran through what I truly felt.

> Me [thinking it through to myself]: I was here because I hated how I was taught. I didn't feel like the teachers cared and I believed that if given the opportunity I could do a better job than what was done for me. A lot of me

felt like I graduated from college based upon how hard I had to work to overcome the gaps that I walked in the door with. In high school we weren't expected to do much. College-ready wasn't the focus. They prepared us to leave and I wanted *out* despite not knowing for sure where I really wanted to go or what I truly wanted for my life. It wasn't until senior year was barreling down on me that I realized a choice had to be made. I just wasn't sure. All I had in my head was a hazy depiction of me getting on a train with a briefcase to do something in a building in a city. The haze never cleared until frustration and a conversation with a good friend of mine, who wanted to be a teacher, led me to convince myself that I too wanted to teach...out of spite.

This was what initially fueled my *why*.

Yet, in front of that panel what I was able to tell them was more or less what every educator says.

Me [in gleeful innocence]: "I want to make a difference."

Thankfully for me, I wasn't asked to flesh out how I might do that. Whatever else they asked I answered with some level of intelligence and honesty.

The Panel [with judgmental optimism]: "Congratulations, Mr. Broadhead. We would love to have you join us."

Excited and optimistic, I accepted the opportunity to teach high school literature. I was fortunate to be considered so quickly after my student teaching experience. It was at the same high school. Yet, being the teacher quickly showed me a difference. The experiences I gained as a student teacher gave me the foundation to feel ready, but those closely monitored moments paled in comparison to having the keys to my own room without anyone sitting in the back watching and silently addressing issues I didn't notice. This was all me, and it was about becoming what I said I wanted for myself when I was in their shoes.

Even though I did not have the best start as a new teacher, my student teaching experience was when I knew I could do the job, even though I hadn't mastered the science to move students forward. I have come to believe that working with kids is the true test to determine how effective you are. That's the beauty and intricacy of teaching. You can go to school and get a degree but doing the job is where you really learn, and depending on your placement, you don't truly know if teaching is what you should be doing. Some don't find out that they shouldn't be a teacher for years and some find out almost immediately. In either case, on the job training is where you know for certain what your career plans really are. My experience provided the glimmer of faith that helped me in my resolve to stay the course, even when I felt doubt.

My teacher mentor was an older white woman named Rochelle Flax. She had been teaching at the school for some time. During the time I was assigned to her she taught a Seniors English Composition and Rhetoric class. I spent only a few weeks observing her and getting to know the students from afar. We spent Sundays working on lesson plans. The process of writing plans took hours. She always asked, "What do you want to teach?" Followed by, "What do you want them to learn?" She showed me a template of how she scripted her lessons. Her method was a dual column headed by TEACHER WILL and

STUDENT WILL.

For example:

| TEACHER WILL | STUDENT WILL |
|---|---|
| Provide notes on author | Take notes and listen attentively |

Under Teacher Will I wrote down everything I planned to do. Under Student Will, I wrote down what I expected the students to do in response to what I was doing. This method forced me to picture myself walking through the lesson and envisioning the class take shape. Once I was done, I aligned the activity and my actions with the standards that were being taught. As I sat scratching my head at the amount of work needed to get through one lesson, let alone a week's worth, I immediately felt heavy. I would watch the sun go down as I sat at Mrs. Flax's kitchen table and shake my head in disbelief. She was very supportive. She told me that in time it would get easier. I took nothing she said for granted because I knew I wanted to be where she was. Although she was at the end of her career, I was infatuated with the level of confidence and content knowledge she had when delivering her lessons. That level of ease was what I longed for. I wanted to experience the click of the switch, or shall I say, the "lightbulb moment," during which I would be on autopilot and students would love to learn from me. But first, I needed to learn how to master developing lesson plans.

In two weeks, whether I was ready or not, she believed I needed to start.

The first lesson I ever taught was poetry. I chose this unit because I experienced a stronger relationship with words through poetry, and felt that helping students to understand emotions through poems would be useful. There was nothing more that fueled my *why* I focused on love. I decided to use sonnets, and approach the concept by creating a scenario where the students try to make a connection with real life to warm up to poetry. The execution of my poem relied heavily upon the participation of the students. I framed the lesson to start with a personal story from me to lighten the mood and set up the student activity. Then I transitioned to what I wanted the students to do to set up the poem while engaging them in the lesson. Lastly, I introduced the poem and work through it for understanding. The first phase went well. The second phase was even better. The students that volunteered to role play did a great job setting up what I hoped the poem would cover, but when I introduced the poem there was a huge wall. None of them understood the poem. The conversation revolved mostly around the language and why it was worded the way it was. The kids' grasp of terms I thought would be easily understood was largely confused, and I spent most of the period looking for ways to help them comprehend the language rather than digging into anything deeper.

In hindsight, I found that I ran into this problem often during my first few years of teaching. I could set the kids up to learn but the meat of the lesson often ran into a wall, and a struggle would ensue until the end of the period. Invariably, the conclusion I often came to was that the students lacked the right foundation to grasp the meaning, or the kids "just didn't want to do the work." It never crossed my mind that whatever wasn't happening during the lesson was driven by some flaw in me.

The correlation between my actions and what students were able to achieve was initially made aware to me during one of my debriefing sessions. This was our practice after I led a lesson. Rochelle was very good at leading by listening and then helping me work through the kinks. She often asked me a series of questions about the lesson and then highlighted what she saw that was good, bad or ugly, to allow me to make adjustments before the next class. During this particular interaction the format was the same but everything she shared hit me differently.

Rochelle: How do you think that class went?

Me [with confidence]: It was pretty good. I didn't get to finish but I thought the class went well.

Rochelle [deadpan]: Really? She paused for a minute. I thought it was the worst lesson you have done.

I was stunned.

Me [making a stupid face because I can't hide my emotions]: Why do you say that?

Rochelle [genuinely asking]: Well, when was Shakespeare's play written?

Me [defending my knowledge of Shakespeare]: 1600's.

Rochelle [raising an eyebrow while methodically landing a gotcha blow]: Then why did you say Middle English?

Me [trying to recall if that was what I said, with another stupid look on my face]

Rochelle [knife revealed]: Well, that was minor but the real question I have for you is: What did you teach? You talked about a lot of things but what was the point?

While she pushed the knife in, I retraced the lesson in my head. She paused for my response and then twisted the knife a little before continuing as she continued.

Rochelle [aka Wicked Witch Judas]: You got pulled off track. The class was talking but there was no learning going on. I was trying to signal to you back here but you didn't notice. You were so busy allowing them to talk to you about other things that you didn't realize you were caught up in a side conversation. I was hoping that you would bring it back but you didn't. You can't forget about your objectives.

Her words arrested the confidence I had amassed in my premature belief that I was getting closer to being a good teacher. I didn't realize that I focused on "the show" and the activity rather than the pedagogy needed to develop learning. The greatest factor that caused me to fall in the trap of the show was my fear that students wouldn't participate. I was happy for *any* participation. I welcomed all conversation and *that part* blinded me from seeing the *teaching part*. I didn't guide the participation so that it could be a fruitful and effective allusion to the lesson rather than a detraction from it. I'd missed the teaching part. Lesson learned.

I got my reps in and in time I slowly gained the confidence to lead the class. I was bumped but not bruised. Rochelle Flax helped me to believe that I had what it took to teach. Her parting words scribed in the literary elements book she gave me as a gift resonated.

*Dear Marcus,*

*Here's something to help you to build your literary resources. In a very short time, I expect to hear about recognitions given to you for excellence in teaching. I will be among the first to brag, "I knew him when. . . ."*

*It's been a pleasure working with you, sharing with you, and learning from you. Even more delightful is knowing I've made a wonderful new friend.*

*Fondly,*

*Rochelle Flax*

I felt like it was a challenge for me to become someone I had not known myself to be, but only hoped I would one day become. It was a wish.

Standing in the classroom as the teacher of record, I felt affirmed in the belief that I could now start my journey to actualize her best wishes. The panel told me I can teach and I believed I was ready.

I thought I was.

The community and school in which I worked were similar to the ones I'd known as a student. On the similarities side, it was a predominantly minority school. But a key difference was the presence of more professional families and traditional family structures. However, the dynamics were beginning to change. I recognized that what may have attributed to a shift in student behaviors and an increase in a growing element of negativity, correlated to home life. It wasn't that parents didn't care or did not support the school or had low expectations for their children. What was happening was a byproduct of what can happen when parents can't afford to live in an area but work very hard to keep their home. It was about the reality that parents were not working a 9 to 5. It was more likely that parents started a second shift, or went to their primary job in the late afternoon through the evening. The absence of parents from the time school let out until about 8 or 9 o'clock at night gave the students very little accountability. Students who were weak enough to succumb to negative choices had six hours to make them. A gang element started to form. The school became a battleground for the differences.

Things started out well for me. I never had a problem with classroom management. I established myself and all my Alpha maleness. The problem was my sense of poor student motivation. I couldn't get them to do homework. I had over 100 students but only 20 or 30 would turn in an assignment, and among those only half turned in a completed one. And only a small fraction turned in something that showed more than a surface response. I provided a ton of feedback after grading papers, just to watch student after student throw what I gave them in the garbage. I took it personally. I assumed it to be a lack of respect for me and/or the care they had for their learning. I could not fathom how they could possibly move beyond high school and become productive if they lacked the motivation to put forth the effort. From my big desk I saw small-minded kids who knew everything yet cared about nothing, and it bothered me.

I'd signed up to make a difference. Remember?

Teaching was supposed to be different. The kids were supposed to be excited to learn. This wasn't the case. I had no clue why and it bothered me. I didn't understand that teaching had layers. I was at the very beginning and did not realize how much of me mattered in the marriage between the science and art of teaching children. And then there was the other stuff...

I chose this town because it was familiar to me. I hung out in this town as a kid and firmly believed (before I started teaching) that being able to relate would be my superpower. By presence alone I thought I should receive respect. In reality, I had authority yet I had not earned respect. Yes. It had to be earned. This was my first lesson. Prior to teaching anything, there were some things I had to do to get the kids to buy into the idea that I *could* teach them anything. More importantly, I had two unspoken hurdles that didn't resonate with my consciousness until a couple of years in the profession. I was a Black male teacher who was young, and who taught English. Pretty obvious. Why the hell should this have taken me two years to realize? I should have had a solid understanding of my role and my presence much sooner, in an eyeblink. I'd considered my optics—my "blackmaleness"—to be a deciding advantage, without considering that, to these kids, I was something new.

Black...not new for them.
Male...not necessarily new for them.
In my twenties...new-ish experience for them.
High school English teacher...not new at all.

Young Black male high school English teacher was BRAND NEW for all, if not most. The department was all women, with me *seeming to serve as the male mascot.* The students had never had a Black male English teacher before, and may never have had an English teacher who was simply male, let alone a man of color. I checked two boxes of unchartered territory. In time, I learned to get used to the relative novelty of my presence.

I was breaking a barrier of expectancy, and some kids struggled to accept it. I often found myself having to prove to the students that I knew what I was talking about, and that the practice I was providing to help them learn was sound. Challenges to me came in the form of, "Mrs. So and So, my teacher from last year, said," and, "Welll, how do *you* know?" Responses of that sort felt like a finger pointed in my face. It happened so often that it became apparent in real time that there was something that made them believe I could not help them as a teacher. Consequently, I went through a period where I had to *prove* that I knew. I had to prove that whatever I put before them could be digested as trusted information that they could believe was factual, despite the source. Although every teacher should, I felt a responsibility to be sure to know every aspect of what I was going to deliver, because I knew I was going to get a question to see if I did, whether they knew the answer or not. Of course I was hurt by this realization. Even though I couldn't blame them I blamed them—but not for long.

> As I sorted through the confrontation, I had to ask myself a couple of questions: Had they interacted with educated Black men before? Yes. In what capacity? What spaces did Black men occupy in their lives, and how might that assist me in *this* space?

My Black male colleagues were predominantly coaches, or an administrator in charge of discipline. That was the kids' reality.

Despite my understanding of that, the level of scrutiny I

received made me more aware of not only what I said but how I handled myself and my projected self-image.

## WHAT I SAID OR DIDN'T SAY

Based upon what I was teaching, I was more attentive about my word choice. No one asked me to do so or coached me to care. It was important to me to be careful with the language I used because I was an English teacher. I didn't use slang or relax my tongue. I didn't want to indict my own credibility to teach. From an objective standpoint, I should not have been using slang and I should have been careful with my word choice. I was a professional. However, my immaturity caused me to use terminology and vocabulary that was beyond them. I was doing my best impression of Michael Eric Dyson before I even knew who he was. I carried an air of "If-you-don't-understand-then-look-it-up," coupled with "I-will-not-dumb-myself-down-for-you" snobbery. Meanwhile, I was missing the point of communicating. Without realizing it, my actions were counterintuitive and alienating. Rather than meeting the kids where they are and building them up, I left them where they were and talked down.

## JEANS DAYS

After being yelled at to leave the teacher's lounge, I had to be more mindful of how I dressed. Fridays were jeans days for everyone but me. The look of professionalism was beaten into my psyche by the Assistant. Superintendent. She had my best interests at heart, while scaring me to death about putting on anything less than the uniform of professionalism. The minimum expectation was a shirt and tie, so I took it a step further and wore a blazer and slacks daily. I accepted this as a proper way to serve as a role model while creating some separation. At 24, I pretty much looked like the kids I was there to teach. My clothes let me optically represent some level of authority in the classroom—and allow me into the teacher's lounge without being mistaken for a student.

In as much as I believed "looking the part" would demonstrate that I was a professional, and to be aspirational for my male students, it worked against me. It put up a wall. I didn't realize that I provided less accessibility to who I truly was, and allowed a representation of who I believed I needed to be to dictate how I interacted with my students. Being young and dumb, I chalked up their indifference to immaturity on their part and leaned into my stance of being a professional. I found myself lying about who I was under the guise of showing them something different.

Student A [in genuine curiosity]: Mr. B! You listen to hip hop?

Me [quickly filtering for relevance to the lesson]: No. Finish your essay.

Student B [in genuine curiosity]: Mr. B! You heard about…?

Me [not listening]: Nathaniel Hawthorne? I heard about him and James Baldwin, so unless you are referring to that I don't know what you're talking about.

Many nights I sat up wondering how to fix education rather than me. I approached each lesson wondering how to get the kids to care. Not once did I realize how I was contributing to the problem. I hit a wall because good intentions could only take me so far. I needed the science of the craft to truly help students attain success in the classroom. Without a teacher mentor, I no longer had someone in the classroom or over my shoulder to bounce ideas off of, or to effectively challenge me. I didn't have anyone to ask. The school had a professional climate of selfish autonomy, and if a colleague asked how everything was going, it was only to determine how much longer I was going to stay rather than an invitation to offer help.

There was more negative banter than there was camaraderie. Well, there was camaraderie in the negative banter. I was already starting to hear the voice of doubt. I didn't need a physical chorus of negativity to amplify what I was beginning to feel.

It was easy for me to isolate myself simply because I did not feel like I had anything in common with colleagues in the English department. And in my isolation, I was left to fend for myself within the walls of my ignorance, while hoping to somehow fix my problem. Although frustrated, I wanted to create better outcomes. At the pit of my stomach there was a sinking feeling because I encountered many students who really didn't see a purpose of school or an education, despite the fact that I was there with my cape on. Everything felt really, really hard.

And this was my first year.

My first year turned into a learning experience. I learned that there was more to education than I'd thought. The business of the classroom is just one part. Getting to know students is the other. I had not yet figured out how to effectively do both those things simultaneously. It was a lot to digest, and thankfully, that's what summers are for. It gave me time to reflect. The year ahead was promising.

I decided to take a different approach. I decided to take the time to provide opportunities to understand my students. I was careful not to take class time to go off topic, but I allowed moments to occur where they had some voice. These interludes were purposely brief, but with them, I began learning how to move from something that was relevant to the students and connect it to the content or skill I was teaching. It wasn't where I wanted it to be or where I ultimately ended up, but it provided a window with which to develop my lessons. Yet in this moment it sparked something a bit more unexpected. Although I was facing similar concerns as the year previously, I began noticing that the students started coming to my room after school.

Darell [pronounced duh-rell]: What you still doing here Mr. B?

Me [sarcastically responding]: Grading these essays that you didn't do.

Darell [caught off guard while laughing]: You got that. You got that.

Very simple back-and-forth dialogue about nothing turned into daily visits from interested kids, and the friends that tagged along. The opening was the same. Some comment focused on surprise that I was in my room at all before sitting down to ask me personal questions. I met students that I didn't have who were brought by those I did have. At times, students who had cut my class earlier that day came to me after school and just sit. After briefly getting on to them about cutting, I'd rhetorically ask, "What do you want?"—knowing that the student most certainly wasn't coming for extra help. It was from these moments that I began connecting with them. Based upon what they shared directly with me, or started to discuss in my presence, I learned how much the community had changed and what kinds of issues the students faced day to day.

I now knew what types of gangs were surfacing and what certain symbols meant. Quite a few of my students were in gangs. It bothered me because when they were in my class I didn't see anything that made me feel like the students were lost or hopeless. All I saw were students that were misguided. The wrong people were holding their attention. Voids of family and connectedness were being filled with gang affiliation, and no matter how much their parents wanted them to do the right thing, they were outnumbered by the abundance of negative opportunities. I found myself repeating the phrase "I don't understand..." during every conversation we had. The worst part is that I had no solution to offer them.

In those moments I was thinking within my role as teacher alone, and couldn't fathom how I could help beyond what I was doing in the classroom. And from this lens, I felt helpless. I heard the words that they were saying about "their why" but beyond thinking: *This is just the dumbest shit I ever heard,* I remained silent while realizing I couldn't relate. The helplessness was unfamiliar. Being this close, I saw beneath the ideal but remained as distant as a voyeur.

Just because we shared the same skin complexion and lived in the area was worth nothing. There was a shift. Their reality was very different from mine. Everything that made sense to them was insane to me and it made me sad.

Given the circumstances, I chose to use the time after school to give advice, break ties in arguments and just be a sounding board for students. It was then that I shared my perspective of what I was hearing them share with me. They were listening. They were attentive and engaging me in deep discussion of the sort I never saw during class. I was delightfully disgusted.

From the interactions with students, a couple of young ladies who wanted to start a Step team asked if I could be their sponsor. My "yes" was naively faster than my comprehension of the commitment, or the process necessary to create the team. I had no idea what it would take beyond knowing how to Step and develop Step shows. It was my understanding that these students wanted me to help them to do something they truly wanted to do and knew enough about me to ask them to help was enough. In that moment, I felt I could help, and wanted to do whatever I could to add some positive energy to the school. I sat with about three young ladies and worked on developing the team's purpose and name before presenting the idea to the principal. All girls. God helped me immensely. Navigating the personalities of 13 young ladies was...special. The time spent was an honor and a blessing. Accepting the responsibility was my way of helping them. However, everything about the experience of working with them and extending myself beyond the classroom helped me.

And just as I began to find my center, I was moved to a feeder junior high school.

I was blindsided. There is a significant difference in levels and I had no idea what I was getting into. I was stunned. Further, I did not know that I could be placed into another grade level. Since I believed I was contributing to the high school by being an advisor/coach of the step team, moving me out didn't seem to make sense. I thought my willingness to be a part of the school as a whole was something that would be noted when decisions about placement took place. I was frustrated because I made a commitment to a group of students. I thought my effort to build school spirit through my involvement with this team should have counted for something. It didn't. I thought I wouldn't be transferred. I was.

At the time, I had no earthly idea how this process took place, and the decision made me feel a bit insignificant. Furthermore, this placement change occurred upon my return after the summer break, so it hit me a bit harder. It was a major transition for me. I was certified in grades 6-12 to teach English but I preferred high school students. I understood them. After all, I wasn't that far removed from the experience. I thought there were things that I could tap into that would prepare them for what awaited them after high school.

Begrudgingly, I packed my things and prepared to teach at the middle school. A part of me was relieved when I found out that the principal was my former high school math teacher, Mr. Ray. I remembered him to be someone that took time to talk to us about some of the issues that were going on at the school. He also had classes on Saturday to help us. I looked up to him and thought it fitting that he held the position as principal. He demonstrated that he would rather do something to make a change rather than complain about the system. I reached out to him immediately and considered him to be a mentor. Mr. Ray was where I thought I would eventually end up, so I paid attention.

While working at the middle school, I was still trying to figure out how to do my job. The age gap was the greatest curve for me. I understood what high school was; seventh grade was a new ball game. The kids felt too far away. I couldn't relate. I couldn't find a common ground of reality to connect myself to them. I found myself repeating myself and unable to complete a sentence without trying to regain a student's attention, so I didn't have to repeat myself a second time. I shouted often to quiet them down and tossed out empty threats as a go-to for classroom management. I often sighed heavily and was overwhelmed by frustration. I had no toolbox to dig into, nothing that would help me feel that what I was doing was working.

Needless to say, moving these young students academically from where they were to where they needed to be was a task. My biggest problem was that I honestly wasn't sure where they needed to be. There wasn't a clear curriculum or guideline that helped me to get them anywhere. In a lot of ways, I was experimenting and hoping for the best. I needed help but couldn't pinpoint where to start. Not knowing was the root of the problem. I had no idea which behaviors were normal for their age, what a healthy struggle should look like, or what were proficient intellectual responses. Each day was a feel in the dark, and at no point did I get a sense of familiarity and comfort. I could only count on negative behaviors. It was difficult to see anything beyond that.

To add insult to my frustration, I was over-observed by Ms. Seigert a district administrator, who was over the English department. I felt tension on each occasion. *Me* and my eyes dared my class clowns to choose any moment during the observation to perform. *They*, waiting for their opening in the cloak of any extended silence on my part. *She,* glaring while moving to make disapproving gestures between note taking, observing me meticulously enough to see the words form on my lips and fall at the feet of the students' desks after futile attempts to penetrate their ears. Jumping out of a window mid-lesson would have been an easy way out of this. Am I exaggerating? No. The windows didn't open and we were on the ground floor.

I had been warned before meeting the woman who would observe me. Ms. Seigert was considered to be pretty meticulous about everything. From the physical setting to what was happening in the classroom, she made notes for correction. She did not disappoint. It was as if she knew these things were said about her. Rather than change, she elected to stand firm in her wickedness. After my first evaluation I was taken aback by all the things she criticized. I knew I wasn't perfect but from what I read I couldn't find solutions to the flaws she identified. I shared the remarks with a colleague who told me I could write a rebuttal. I didn't. Still, I felt that she just didn't like me, or couldn't communicate well enough for me to understand that what she was saying was not personal and had merit. The level of criticism I received from her bothered me but I couldn't articulate what I needed because I was still trying to understand where I fit in, and what I needed to do at my new school. I held off from asking Mr. Ray for his advice and looked to solve my own problems.

It wasn't too long before I received another observation. Seigert's comments were worse, and at this time they felt personal. According to the evaluation, students were not learning and the class was in utter chaos. The remarks read in such a way that she should have intervened at the moment of the observation.

This time I decided to write a rebuttal. I asked my Union rep to read it as a second pair of eyes. She suggested changes prior to my submission. I made them and submitted my rebuttal, and quickly forgot about it. A few days passed before I was asked to come to the principal's office for a meeting. I arrived to see Ms. Seigert and Mr. Ray. Seigert started the conversation by stating that she was appalled by my response, and that she basically disagreed with what I said. She highlighted specific points I'd made in my rebuttal. As she spoke, I wasn't too sure of what my response should've been at that moment, but I felt uneasy. My gaze shot to Mr. Ray to gain some sort of clarity. He averted his eyes. No relief. I knew it was wrong for this conversation to take place at all, simply because I'd been called in to be yelled at for something that was within my right to do. Collecting my thoughts, I reiterated to the chairperson that I was simply asking her for her help, since she appeared to have all the answers. I told her that her evaluation pointed out flaws without support, and without ideas to rectify what was wrong. She was visibly bothered when I suggested that she provide the assistance. At various points in her rebuttal to my rebuttal she repeated the phrase "I know these kids..." and each time it stung. At the time I took offense because she was a white woman *and* she wasn't a teacher. I couldn't imagine how she could possibly know my students better than I did. I took offense because of the way she said "these kids." It was formed in a matter of generalization, as if to emphasize the notion that if she had ever taught Black children before, then she knew what all black children needed. For me, the students that stared back at me were the students I had to get to know and teach. Since Seigert was not in the classroom with the children I was currently teaching, there was no way she could tell me that she knew *these kids*. I knew she didn't. She was a visitor who never taught my kids and her confidence in her indignation bothered the shit out of me.

When the meeting was done I felt heavy.

Thankfully, the discussion occurred before my lunch break, so I had some time to get myself together before I taught again. I decided to speak with Mr. Ray to understand what I did wrong, and get to direction. During the meeting with Ms. Seigert he'd said very little, if anything, so I didn't get a sense of where he stood. I wanted to know. Candidly, I asked him why the meeting occurred the way it had. Blankly, he shook his head and told me in a disappointed tone that I should've never submitted a statement.

I was confused.

Even after I expressed my confusion, Mr. Ray couldn't tell me why I should have kept my reactions to myself. It was as if the reason why wasn't something he could reveal. In that moment everything I thought about him changed. I didn't understand the dynamics or hierarchy, but I'd thought that he might offer me more than what I received. I wanted guidance from him, to help me to be better, but I received none. I had expected from him something he had no intention of providing. It didn't dawn on me then that I'd cast him in the role of mentor, a role which he'd never asked for, and certainly never audibly accepted.

I placed the responsibility of Black male role model on him, before stopping to consider that it may not ever have been in him to be one for me or for anyone else. Who he no longer was in my head made me dislike him for destroying the idea of him. He called me into his office.

Mr. Ray [spoken as if it hurt him]: I am not going to renew your contract next year.

I was stunned into silence, yet my facial expression spoke non-stop.

Mr. Ray [speaking as if to break through the acknowledgment of my feelings]: You have too many failures.

Me [confused]: Failures? Yeah...they failed. They didn't do anything. They wouldn't turn in work. What was I supposed to do?

Mr. Ray [as if he was actually answering my question]: Either way you have too many. You can't fail them.

If my head could explode at this statement, it would have. Up until this moment, I'd had no idea that this concern was a thing. I had in no way formulated in my mind that if a student failed my class, despite my attempts to help them to pass, that I would ultimately be held responsible. None of this made sense to me. I sat there stunned. Without much thought, I asked a follow-up question that I felt was a bit rhetorical and farfetched. I was not prepared for the response.

Me [trying not to curse]: So I'm supposed to just pass them even though they didn't do the work?

Mr. Ray [as a matter of fact]: No one is going to hire you with that high of a percentage of failures. You will not be able to keep a teaching job if you fail them.

Me [W…T…F]: So just pass them?

Mr. Ray [with finality]: If you want to keep your job.

The conversation we had was defining, and it shaped my perception of what I thought education was supposed to be. Although I knew I didn't have the answers and had a long way to go before I could reach the level of excellence I wanted to have as a teacher, I knew that what I had hoped to do wasn't in alignment with what the principal was telling me. My heart sank. Here sat a man that I'd looked up to. I thought he cared for me and my development as a new educator. What I once believed about him I no longer recognized. He didn't help me to understand what I needed to know to help kids. Worse, when the Ms. Seigert came in he did nothing to support or protect me. If I had asked him why he let me go I am sure he would have told me I'd given him no choice. The fact of the matter is that he had many choices to make but he was choosing himself over me. In myself I saw someone who wanted to do well by children, and was open to learn how to be more effective. From him there was no investment. It was then that I held firm to the conclusion that I didn't matter. And because he made me feel that way, I hated him. Because of what I encountered I *hated* him. He had my dreams and all that I worked for in his hands and he chose himself.

I
*hated*
him.

Too strong? No.

I was hurt by this experience, and truly did not understand those who worked in education. Frustrated by the circumstance, I blamed people rather than the educational system for the failures I witnessed. I told myself that I would try to become a teacher in another town. Then, depending on what happened at my next employment, I'd make a decision about my future. I was prepared to quit the profession despite not having a clue about any other professional option. All I went to school to do was to teach, and there was no neon light pointing in the direction of a viable option. The only flicker was what I believed I was supposed to do as a teacher. I told myself that wherever I landed next was going to be my last stop in education. I was angry but I wanted one more environment to help me to see education in another light. I didn't want to believe that everything I went to school for was a lie. I needed a new opportunity, a different perspective, a chance to do what I intended--somewhere--anywhere to reassure me that I didn't make a mistake.

Well, not exactly "anywhere." I didn't go too far.

# FREEPORT

In my search for another place to continue my career, I looked at places that I felt were familiar to the communities I believed needed me. It never crossed my mind to work in a town that was majority white. A lot of me believed that I somehow was not living up to what I set out to do if I went to serve in a predominantly white community. A part of me believed that I was not allowed to.

I went with a frat brother's sisters to a job fair in a neighboring system. At the time she was looking to be in administration and I was looking to be wanted. Fortunately, I was given a callback and after many rounds of interviews I was hired. I was among four men in the department and was also the only Black male. I noticed but it bothered me less than my initial awareness of being the only Black male. There were some good people in the department, and unlike the previous placement I connected with more teachers there. Although we were coming from various backgrounds, what we did have in common was our age. I had a sense of camaraderie, which allowed me to navigate through the culture of the school. Instead of being trapped inside my own head about what was or wasn't happening, I felt comfortable bouncing ideas off of my dept. colleagues or talking through my observations with a few people in other departments.

This high school was in transition. However, the school was no longer a direct reflection of the children that lived in the community. The village was an economically diverse suburb which was originally considered an oystering community. Owning a boat was not an abnormality and waterfront property was a staple. Over a couple of decades there was an increase in the Latino and African American population. Although, there white families throughout the community, sending their children to private schools was the viable alternative.

Those who were there before me could speak of what was now coming undone, and what the expectations used to be. Multiple changes in leadership began to expose gaps in a culture of expectations by all that could sustain leadership shifts. The principal who hired me did not last after the first year and neither did the superintendent. The energy was shifting. I could tell that what this school once was began forming into something different. The students began to have more conflict, which disrupted learning. The staff noticed. There was an expectation for something to be done by administration and when it did not come it appeared that expectation of change morphed into lowered expectations. The negative behavior of students washed over and was dismissed as the DNA of minority teens. I didn't subscribe to this belief. I knew this system had been stronger when I was growing up and it bothered me to hear complainers that did very little, if anything, to provide a solution. Every faculty meeting focused on labor disputes and issues surrounding benefits and changes that threatened retirement. Nothing was ever discussed about the safety of students or building back up the rigor and standards. It was always about bureaucracy. Although I attended the meetings out of compliance, I dreaded them, and invariably wanted to walk out. None of what was discussed seemed to matter, and it became evident to me that what I was experiencing is what education truly is about. This was a new lens for me and it was disheartening to grasp and accept. My idea of what education was supposed to be was feeling more and more like an unattainable ideal rather than a possible reality. The noise from the adults was too loud. In Union meetings, I often found myself asking, "What are we even talking about and why does everyone seem to really care about this?" It was all just empty or angry or both. And that question forced me to ask another question that often hurts while on the journey of trying to answer it: "What are we really doing?"

Even though my ability to teach was taking shape, the pocket of comfort and reward I sought had yet to materialize within the classroom. I wasn't certain about was being taught or how it was being received, or how anything we were doing was helping kids in the way I thought education should. I began to understand the disconnect students felt and worked to find meaning for them. There were times where I felt like I made that link but those moments was few and far in between. On other days it was merely about getting through the lesson. I'd survived another day. And this was unacceptable. Having recognized that there was still a disconnect, I retreated to what provided a connection that I longed for within the classroom. I tossed the Mr. B hat off and I volunteered my time working with an organization that utilized the activity of Stepping as a vehicle to reinforce the message of being drug free. The team was housed at the school and included about ten male students. The time I spent working with them was fulfilling. I gained insight into who they were and I shared relevant aspects of myself. These young men had varied backgrounds, but wanted to do the right thing and represented themselves well. I did not feel like I was there to fill some hole left by an absentee father. My role was more like the cool uncle. Working with them helped to shape my sensibility further, and provided the balance I needed between my role as a teacher and coach. Having maintained this balance, I accepted that my role as a coach would serve as what I longed to feel as a teacher. Given my professional experiences so far, I was resigned to the belief that what I set out to achieve would be limited to the relationships I formulated adjacent to my role as a teacher.

Despite the negativity that was taking shape in the school, what I was a part of helped bring me to a more hopeful perspective on what could be done to combat things observed but unchecked. Before my role as a teacher, I never formally held a position as a mentor. I'd been asked to look out for this one's li'l cousin and so-and-so's younger brother but I had not considered a formal mentorship. I always looked at teaching as filling that function. My work as a step coach didn't strike me as true mentorship, either. It was indirect and organic. Standing at this point, I felt I needed to do more, but was unsure of what "more" looked like.

I often spoke casually with a colleague about what we were observing. We shook our heads. We related what we were seeing to our personal experiences growing up. We questioned inaction on the part of the administration and then we shook our heads some more.

In the meantime, I noticed that another staff member took a different approach and decided to do something to address the issues. Rather than complain about her disappointment, she created an opportunity to teach female students to avoid what she believed to be harmful behavior. The organization was called LADY. She brought women in to teach etiquette and to expose the female students to all aspects of conduct that are becoming in a young lady. The staff member was the school nurse. Of all people to decide to do something, it was the school nurse! She showed me that *anyone* with the passion and willingness to commit can affect positive change. No pecking order or hierarchy appointed her to take charge. As long we were adults and worked at the school, we all had the right to take responsibility for the children who attended. She showed me that making a difference did not have to come from a systematic change but from something at the ground level. I admired her for what she did.

When I commended her for her work, she suggested that I should lead the male version of the program. She offered the name GENTS. Her confidence in me made me feel good about who I was as a human being, and helped me believe I was the right person for the program. How could I say she was mistaken? My ego accepted the possibility of developing a program for the young men at the school. The timing made sense and it was a great opportunity to force me to put my ideas to work and to stop complaining. I had the power to do something. For me, this was extremely exciting because it offered me an intentional approach to make a difference in a way that had motivated me before I entered education. What was also taking shape was my understanding of what so-called formal education was missing. Quite a few things that truly mattered were never broached within education. All of the things that caused a student to ask sardonically "What does this have to do with me?" was what would fill out the curriculum created for this program. I wanted to provide kids the opportunity to learn from the missteps that I had lived through.

Even though I was young and still learning, I was fortunate enough to have experienced some obstacles that gave me the right to highlight better choices while presenting students with resources that might lead to better choices. However, I was smart enough to realize that I couldn't do this alone, so I asked one of my colleagues who shared my frustration to commit to develop the program and deliver workshops for our young men. We decided that the programs would be open to all male students, and take place monthly, after school. I recognized that the students may not have considered the organization cool enough to join, so our approach was to treat it like "church." Noncommittal. Lure them in based upon issues related more closely to kids' lives and see how many we can get to keep coming back. Those who regularly returned would become our first group. This was our plan.

In the first year we talked the young men about building financial wealth, making positive choices, how to properly pursue relationships, protecting yourself and making healthy choices regarding sex. We discussed how to enter the music industry, interview skills, and the controversy of using the N word. Depending upon the topics, we had good to great turnouts. We were filling a gap. We were making a difference beyond the students we taught. I was feeling full, and I loved every aspect of what was developing based upon what we created out of a suggestion.

After the first year of implementing the program, I was moved to the feeder middle school.

Yes, I was mad as hell...*again.*

A lot of the feelings I once had about being placed in a middle school after my first year at my previous school were coming back. This change was after being at the school for two years so it hit harder. Despite my frustration, my change of placement came with a sense of relief because the new principal, Mr. Lee, was someone I worked with at my former middle school.

Prior to becoming a teacher, I worked at a temp agency and filled a long- term secretary opening at my former middle school. As luck would have it, I supported Lee along with another assistant principal. It was his first appointment and during the time of my assignment he served indirectly as a mentor. The nature of the work allowed me to shadow and interact with him often and since I was pursuing education I took the liberty of asking questions to get a sense of his journey. In a short period of time we got cool *enough*. Although we didn't stay in touch after the temp position was over, I knew him well enough to feel reassured that my transition would not result in disappointment.

Fortunately for me, Mr. Lee did support me, but unlike the way I'd imagined. While I worked under his leadership, we had an interaction that was a moment of brutal honesty. In no way did I love the interaction in real time. As I write this, the clarity of his intention is evident, but in the moment I had to go experience many emotions to arrive at "appreciative." Today I am extremely appreciative. Eighteen years ago...not so much. He helped me to snap out of the funk I was living in after being transferred. In one rip...

I cannot remember whether the conversation was prompted by a general interaction where I took the liberty to be candid about how I was feeling regarding my transfer, or if the moment developed from a meeting I was having with him about a student issue that resulted in me being sucker punched. In either instance I know how it ended.

Mr. Lee [as if having thought about this for some time]: ... You walking around here mad everyday ain't gonna change anything. You're here now. You gotta get over it. Right now!

Me [watching the air escape from lungs]: The shot was to the body. There I was, doubled over.

I easily thought of things I expected him to say instead that would provide comfort. Easily ten other things that all started with "Yeah, that's foul" and ended with. "I will see what I can do."

Nope!

Mr. Lee [insert straight face and taunting look]: Get over it! He yelled often when asserting his point. He added nothing more to soften the words around what he meant. He left it hanging there in front of me, to swallow whole. Daring me to ignore it or accept it.

This was my first lesson in recognizing the power of a mindset. I had heard the concept of changing your frame of mind but it never seemed real enough for me to apply it and mean it. I was never challenged to accept a thing mentally and allow my actions to follow. I was mad *today* I needed to change my attitude about my circumstance *tomorrow.* All I was afforded was a chance to sleep on it and sulk prior to falling asleep. But come the next morning, I needed to have fully accepted and had a funeral for the negative attitude that I harbored.

Miraculously, it worked. It worked because I quickly came to realize that I was embarrassed. I was embarrassed because my visible pouting was apparent to others. My negativity was evident, which means my students felt it as well. I wasn't giving this placement a chance, and in turn I really wasn't giving my kids what they deserved. Because children are not fools, they weren't going to make it easy for me. Any pushback I received was because they knew my heart wasn't there for them. I was so busy in my head that I did not realize how much my energy and demeanor mattered. The best indicator that the students were not working for me was when I had come to a point where I believed I needed help and asked, Mrs. Freidman, the English Language Arts coordinator, to come and observe, to see what support she could offer.

I was certain that she would throw her hands up as well, but the very opposite occurred. She offered to teach the class. I sat my butt down and, boy, did I get a show. Mrs. Freidman had them everywhere she wanted them to be in the lesson. She was funny. She made connections to them. She spoke their language in the sense that she understood their references and what kids their age cared about, and then she tied everything together. Not one disruption. Not one student pushing back. And then she turned it back over to me. After that display, I didn't *want* it back. She did more in one lesson and with more ease than I'd managed in any of what I would call my best moments teaching. Mrs. Freidman was a gray-haired, petite Jewish woman and she...*knew* my kids.

The students saw that she cared and was interested in them. Her demeanor mattered. Her tone mattered. Her entire approach was geared toward what the lesson needed to be for them. In my frustration and discomfort with the change, I was teaching the material and not the children. I had not yet understood how to validate who they were and make it become important enough to incorporate into my delivery of the material. This was lost on me, and it was further buried by my indignation that I was there in the first place. It was this experience that crystallized the impact that my attitude had on my teaching. And because of this recollection of how I was stopping my students from having a rewarding experience, I immediately got over it.

Was I immediately an awesome teacher? No. But the right wheels were turning and I was committed to being better. Because I saw better from someone I didn't expect, I knew that better was possible. It was going to take time, but I was learning.

I decided to bring the mentorship program I started at the high school down to the middle school. The kids and I took a walking trip to the bank to help them understand why they needed a bank account. We provided them with bags and organizers. We gave them a safe space to communicate and share. We provided them with information and experiences they needed if they were to succeed. The only difference between my intention at this level versus the high school was that the information I gave to the younger kids was delivered as cautionary tales, and was intended to be preemptive. At times, I pulled all the young men that had to serve detention into my room to listen and participate in the workshop as a form of recompense for whatever had them serving their "time." This approach was gentler than what I'd done at the high school, where we wanted students to willingly attend and participate.

The conversations with these young men were a gateway for me to connect with them as a man. I got to be me, and it was a side of me that they never saw. The *me* they got to see in this context had a tone of genuine care and concern. That guy was interested in where they were from and their journey. He listened to their perspectives, listened intently, asked more questions to understand more clearly, and then offered a different perspective with the hope they'd make better choices when the time came.

My door was now open to them. We talked about all sorts of things; I was willing to argue with them that Dipset was an awful rap group in comparison to my list of favorites. My commitment shifted back to where it needed to be. When I had a rough class period, I stopped and asked for help. There were more moments when I took a deep breath or stopped everything to request that we, as a class, take a moment to focus. There was more direction and intention in my articulation of our why: "Because of the importance of..." "Because in the long term this will help...." All of which was now predicated upon trust.

My craft still needed work but I became a stronger teacher due to this shift. The moments after school, talking about life with students, breathed life back into me. Education wasn't all I had thought it to be, but what I was *making it* to be was worth me being in it. I knew that without the opportunity to teach kids (no matter how awful I believed I was doing), I would never have gained the perspective I needed to support students beyond the classroom.

This was the beginning of something. I was finding my place. It was during this time that I became aware enough to realize that I had to find a way to transfer the worth of what I was doing after school to *during* school. Somehow. At the time I wasn't smart enough. I was only wise enough to realize I didn't know how to marry the two. Yet, because GENTS existed I didn't have to worry about what I couldn't figure out as a teacher. I was fulfilling my obligation and making a difference after school. This was a medium that allowed me to remain in education despite the feeling I had at the pit of my stomach. The "pit" housed the fear that my choice to pursue education was a wrong one. What I felt was missing in me as a classroom teacher gnawed away at me. I felt better overall but I could not recognize my growth as an educator. GENTS gave me value and connected me to the profession. Without it, I would have quit. That would have been a new journey and a different book. With it I gained an understanding that led me to clarity and the ability to be the teacher I always wanted to be. I ultimately left New York, and worried that the kids I wanted to be great for wouldn't fully benefit from the fruits of my journey. I worried that the students I left might harbor the notion that I'd quit.

## THE TAKEAWAY

What I had experienced over the first six years of my teaching career made a significant impression on me. The challenges I faced, while navigating within the schools and the systems, introduced different variables I hadn't initially considered. In six years I worked at four different schools in two different districts. There was a leadership change in both systems, either from the district office or originating within the school I was serving. The idea of change and the tension that lives in not knowing what is to come, under new leadership, was constantly on the minds of the staff. In every instance it adversely affected the school as a whole and students were on the receiving end. As a teacher, whatever I was not receiving from administration by way of support or understanding, negatively impacted the classroom. Multiply this scenario by all educators in the building. There was an absence of consistency that led to a void of accountability. My experiences revealed to me that some teachers got into the profession because it provided a job and it was convenient. Some teachers were only motivated to do right by children based upon mandates or what the unions could not protect them from. My experience thus far showed me that there were administrative practices that had no real merit or rationale, other than the fact that a practice or procedure needed to be put in place to have something to defer to when common sense or logic is sparse. My experiences in this environment revealed a level of apathy by children and adults at depths that I never knew existed. I could understand firsthand how the weight of the work can be burdensome at times, but to live in a daily funk and function out of compliance was a wrinkle I'd never expected to exist in more than one system.

There was also the reality that the world our students lived in did not stop when they attended school. There was no escape, and no matter how engaging I made my lessons, my efforts paled in comparison to what peered at the kids from between the blinds. For an educator to face the students' collective reality, and find the right approach to deliver the content while avoiding biases formed from their own values, seemed an insurmountable task. In this environment, every teacher had to learn how to combat deep-seated issues that exist in the world, and find solutions to allow for classroom learning to happen. No teacher program taught a class on how to develop a sanctuary for learning. And if such a need was recognized, it was not by formal design but because of the moral and thoughtful obligation of the teacher who saw the need. The greater the need for survival in the community, when mated to a school's failure to address that need, the greater the difficulty of educating children. There were teachers in this environment who initially meant well, but the unattended variables consistently presented themselves. For many, facing this was too much to bear. Education for most was a lifelong career that was entered with retirement in mind. But in truth, education was a commitment in sweat equity. To know that the labor required to make a difference was the equivalent of being asked to turn a mountain into rubble with a pair of scissors burdened some teachers with feelings of hopelessness and frustration. For those arrested by these feelings, whatever they chose from this point forward lived in the spirit of survival and what that may look like would adjust as retirement approached. Talking to some of the teachers in this environment was emotionally exhausting because it suggested my own possible fate. At what point would I, too, surrender to a belief that nothing I could do made a difference? What more could I *really* do, and does anyone care that must be done? Is there a plan for these children and if so, what is the intended outcome? Is this chaos the plan? Will things ever change? Could they? Should *things* change or should I? What if I am the only one? Why is it this way? Is this what education is about?

The whirlwind of questions led to me to make a choice that was in conflict with what I believe I entered education to do. I wanted to support young Black boys, and provide opportunities for learning that would spark Black children to want more and do more for themselves. And now I was leaving, and taking part of the solution with me. A piece of me carried guilt. I felt like I was selling out. I was leaving the trenches where the issues resided. I was walking away from the work that needed to be done for *my* people. I was abandoning the mission before I could see the results of the work that I had begun to do. Furthermore, there were not many Black men in the schools where I worked, and I felt obligated to fill a void. Yup! All by myself. I still champion this belief, but I no longer minimize my importance in a predominantly white school, or to any child who is not Black.

The second act of my teaching career was the complete opposite of what I had previously experienced. I moved forward with intentionality. For all of the questions and concerns that I had about majority-minority schools and my place within them, I sought the answers over the next six years while working in a predominantly white school setting. It was here where I gained the answers to some of my unanswered questions, and unearthed new elements that encouraged student success. More importantly, I grew.

## LESSON LEARNED: INVEST IN CHILDREN NOT IN CONTENT

I made an assumption. In this environment I believed I automatically was going to make a difference because I showed up. I didn't make an investment in understanding who my students were so I could teach them. My presence alone was not enough. I was unable to transfer my investment in children the minute I was faced with having to deliver content. My lesson plan was developed from the question: How am I going to teach this? —when it should have been developed from the question: Based upon what I know about my kids; how can I make this matter? Far too often I neglected to figure out who my audience was. For a teacher, the classroom is one big stage, and every period there's a new audience. My energy mattered to the students, but without connecting to them there was no way I could authentically be the vehicle to properly present content and support the kids' learning process. Who I was as a man was important to them, and I thrived in my support of them beyond the classroom. The real-talk moments that took place after school, formally and informally, were when I connected best. And because of these moments, I have lifelong connections with students I had in my classes, and with some that I never taught but who hung out in my room after school. I was not who I hoped to be as a teacher for them, but, in some way, I was what I needed to be for those kids. They taught me more about myself as an educator that I ever could have learned without them.

What I find to be a struggle for new teachers, and for some veterans, too, is an inability to authentically connect with their students and then use that connection to teach. As educators we insist that relationships are important but sometimes the commitment to the relationship is where the rubber meets the potholes in the road. The idea of relationship building sounds good but an effective educator develops lessons that are driven by relationships. To what extent will the educator consider what they understand about their students to find ways to support every student through the learning process? If the educator teaches from the root of relationship building, then the lessons will be more dynamic. Educators inclined that way organically take risks, shift their perspective and audit what they are doing. They challenge the why of their content before moving forward with a curriculum they haven't carefully thought about. Through my observations of teachers, I have concluded that there are educators who love their subject but have a simple, highly codified Likert-scaled approach to how they feel about the students they teach. For such a noble profession, one can ask how could this be? From the outside looking in, it seems ludicrous for a teacher to enter and stay in a profession without caring for students. Nonetheless, this can be the case. Consequently, it is important for every educator to take stock of each year and reflect upon their practices. He or she must take a hard look in the mirror and ask tough questions. One of the most important questions I ask myself daily is: "How did I connect today?" Although this question takes on a personal meaning for me in light of how I define my purpose, it is a useful question to ask of any educator with a core belief that he or she is in the profession to make a difference. I often say that we are in the heart business. The entry point of our ability to teach, and a student's willingness to be taught by you is the heart. If the educator cannot figure out how to win the battle of the heart, the child's perspective on the teacher, and how they believe you feel about them, will overshadow their ability, and become a roadblock to their achievement. The exponential power of an educator lives in how positive he or she can make students feel about themselves long after the bell rings and the year ends. Attention must be paid to the intentionality that drives connections, and supports student growth.

# TO SIR...WITH LOVE

Teaching in a predominantly white school was a significant change for me. Walking into a scenario where I felt Black with a cape on, I decided that it was more important to listen than to speak. What I mean by this is that everything about my surroundings was new. I had a great deal of respect for the transition I was making. Although I technically was not a new teacher, this change was significant enough to let me accept what I didn't immediately understand, and to be more amenable to my surroundings, rather than to try to force my new environment to bend to me. Throughout my teaching career I have always been the only Black male in my department. Being in a predominantly minority school did not bring me the comfort of knowing that other colleagues looked like me, or were of a similar age, and able to help me walk through my professional growing pains. I absorbed the journey in isolation and made peace with the fact that Black males are not entering education at the same rate as Black women, or staying in the profession as black women, and white teachers of both genders.

I stood out more in this setting because there were more boxes to check that set me apart from my colleagues and my students.

Prior to this setting I wore my attributes as a matter of fact:

Young.
Black.
Male.
English teacher.

Within this setting my attributes felt like an announcement:

YOUNG
BLACK
MALE
ENGLISH TEACHER????
NEW YORKER

I was the collective embodiment of every singular pre-conceived notion that can be made by the staff and students. There was a lot of me to figure out just to place me in a box. Every interaction felt like an interview and I felt pressure in every action and word. I was either going to uphold a generalization or add color to a preconceived notion. I was never speaking for myself when talking with colleagues. I knew that I was well-placed. Because of who I was, colleagues asked questions they'd never asked before. Further, the questions were often preceded by awkward disclaimers intended to assure me that the questions were inspired by more than just my ethnicity. Get it? I accepted the discomfort and welcomed any question. I accepted that who

I am was going to shape how they thought about Black men. All of us. I wasn't going to be abrasive if I was offended but I most certainly was going to bring caution to judgment and provide perspective when there was none.

As the only male in the department, I was the only one with my viewpoint. Although I never felt silenced, and appreciated how I was made to feel a part of the team, I felt distanced from this veteran group of women that had found considerable success at the school. But they were very willing to provide support through resources and lesson plans, and never gave me any negative energy. Those with whom I shared a classroom during my first year were great neighbors. I was not made to feel I could not share the space even though I was only in the room for one period. I was appreciative of their hospitality because it was genuine.

Armed with what I had begun to learn from my previous placement, I began differently in this one. Teaching in this environment let me take the time to share with the kids who I was before I asked them to complete their first assignment. I typed up a letter that spoke to where I had been and what I hope to provide for them, and gave them the letter to bring home to their parents. I struck first. I did not want to start without focusing on who I was. By doing that, I could begin to know who my students were. Give and take. I approached learning by creating lessons that could be easily relatable, even if the circumstance of the text did not directly impact the students. I searched for the honesty or the outrage needed to spark an investment in what we were doing.

I set out to get students to think about ELA after the bell

rang. Each lesson I planned was intended to stimulate the kids to talk about their classroom experience in the halls, and during our next time in class. I wanted learning to resonate. Of course, not every lesson did, but that was the goal, and with each lesson I taught, I was learning how to be a better teacher. I was invested in figuring out how to make my students enjoy my class. They were responsive to what I asked of them; it provided me the right energy to consider more ways to engage them.

The challenge I felt in this environment was driven by proving to myself that I could teach. I felt a pressure (which I placed on myself) to be a teacher who was talked about for how well I taught. I didn't want to just be the cool teacher who dressed well but didn't teach students anything. I wanted to matter because I provided substance. I made this something to shoot for, and used what I was beginning to understand about my students as the entry point to help them to connect.

Students continued to hang out in my classroom. It was there that I learned more about the school community, student concerns, and their feelings as a whole. More importantly, students came by to get clarity on a lesson, or have me take a look at a paper they were writing before it was due. I admired that there was a level of care and ownership in their learning. I recognized there was a dominant culture among the students to perform academically. Doing well was an expectation. Students talked about their school work and spent time in the library or a coffee house in study groups prior to exams. There was a collegiate maturity about their "performance." They sought first to understand how to get the grade that they wanted. Some were willing to rewrite papers and do extra credit as long as there was a chance for their average to go up. Initially, I admired this. I appreciated knowing that there were teenagers who had a mindset of achievement and did not like getting anything lower than a B, and that some looked crushed if they received a B on an assignment. This was new. Other than a brief experience as an adjunct professor, I'd never encountered this sort of student commitment. Outside of feeling like a teacher in a Disney film, I unexpectedly began to be disappointed by their motivation. After a few years it dawned on me that everything that they did was for a grade. For some, learning was not a part of the equation. Getting an A was king, and students' every action was about getting one. The class experience could be great and they could have a healthy struggle and be challenged and be better than they were before they got to the class, but if the time spent did not result in an A, then taking the class was—to them—a mistake, and he or she should have taken another class that would have guaranteed them an A.

After I accepted the job I told myself that if I ever started to complain about the school, I would definitely quit. Yet here I was starting to feel unnerved by this growing clarity about the kids' intentions. I was bothered partly because I chalked up their actions as disingenuous and self-serving. I believed that an A should be the result of how deeply and intently a student analyzed the content and provided fresh ideas. I would not award an A based upon checking boxes and regurgitation. I wanted them to care. I wanted them to aim for more than just a right answer. Upon realizing that most interactions were only a means to this end, I was disappointed.

My notion was further solidified during a parent conference involving student I adored. She was personable and bright, and asked great questions. She was enthusiastic and wanted to do well. Much to my amazement, I was blindsided when the parents began talking down to me and intimated that I was misusing my power as an educator to hurt their child's average, and thus damaging their child's future. At the time of the conference, the student had a B average. I was stunned. I couldn't believe that this was a conversation. The tension was thick and these parents wanted my head. We were having two different conversations. I was leaning into the significance of learning while they would hear none of my nonsense. And with each response to their questions and concerns, unknowingly I dangled my neck out in front of them.

I was told I made my class harder than it needed to be, and was hurting their child's future. The notion struck me as hyperbole. To them...it was a reality. That their child had received her first B was cataclysmic, and contrary to the trajectory of the life they'd chosen for her. At various points, her dad said "How will she get into Harvard?" Perfection was on their path, and there I was, standing in the way of it all.

When the school counselor asked, their daughter said she loved the class. Their child and I had a great relationship. None of this mattered. With passion and exhaustion, her parents declared I was ruining her life. I kindly asked if I could be excused from the meeting. It was clear to me that there was nothing more that needed to be said or done here.

This wasn't the only conference with that type of focus. But because it was the first, it was the most startling.

One question my kids invariably asked about an assigned task cemented my understanding of what was most important to them: "Is this going to be graded?" The grade, above all else, was paramount. I didn't understand but it was becoming abundantly clear why the preoccupation with grades was so important.

Grades were king to their parents, and invariably became their ruler. Have you ever driven behind a car with a bumper sticker that says *My son/daughter is an honor student*? As much as you wanted to ram that car into oncoming traffic, you didn't. For the same reason you may have had that urge to succumb to temporary insanity, the driver of that car was a parent to one of my students. It's one thing to be proud of your child for achieving, but an environment of constant demands and pressure is another.

For many of these students, the spoken expectation was perfection. Making straight A's was a part of bragging rights in the supermarket aisle. It was the precursor to college acceptance letters and potential majors. It was a badge of "better than" that pressured most students to believe that it was their responsibility to live up to. In many cases, the pressure finally became too much too bear. The kids shared with me that they carried a level of stress that just wasn't fair for children (I often thought they forgot that they were children). So much weight was embedded in a test score. With each grade received, the students took a blow to their self-esteem, or exhaled a sigh of relief, and enjoyed a temporary moment of satisfaction. Not getting the desired grade added another hour to whatever study ritual they endured, while they beat themselves up for not doing as well on the last exam as they'd hoped.

Meanwhile, some of my colleagues (not exclusive to the English Department) wore the reputation of having a tough class as a badge of honor. Most educators feel that his or her class is of the utmost importance. Consequently, each provides assignments on top of assignments on top of projects on top of presentations, with drop-dead deadlines. If you were unfortunate enough to drop dead your mom better bring that assignment on your behalf as your dying wish. God forbid receiving a zero, which was sometimes the result if work was not turned in on the due date. In other cases, the student would be penalized a certain amount of points for every day that the assignment was not turned in. The environment created in preparation for college told kids that there was no excuse for work not to get done, and no excuse not to perform well, no matter the number of assignments that needed to be completed.

This was the pressure that we created as a school.

No excuses. Just get it done.

And they did.

They did so while suffering from depression and anxiety. Some self-medicated. Some cut themselves. Some participated in other destructive behaviors. Some fought through and performed, while enjoying the challenge. Some immersed themselves in athletics and the arts in order to cope.

And everyone was "fine."

I began to realize that although a huge economic gap separated my school in New York from the one I presently worked at, students at both schools shared similarities, relative to their realities, that manifested as challenges and pain. What I witnessed initially was as unreal and shocking to me as the first time I found out that Clair Huxtable was a lawyer and Heathcliff was a doctor. This place was as far away from my experience that it was hard to grasp as a reality. This school community was an After School Special. No physical violence. No street danger. Real soccer and cheer moms. They had supper at a designated time. A student parking lot larger than the one for faculty. Holidays and weekends spent at a lake house or any destination a Delta plane could take them. Yet there was as much pain cloaked in Mom's homemade s'mores as there was in the edibles. I didn't know that this much pain existed until I asked.

I took pride in building relationships, and took some liberties during the class period to find out who my students were through writing prompts. So leading up to this particular day, it was not far-fetched for me to ask them to share how they were feeling, or think about a topic that was not traditionally academic. Two students took their lives about a month between each other. This was a first for me. Unfortunately, within the span of my career at this point, the unfortunate and untimely deaths of teenagers through car accidents or violence at the hands of someone else occurred enough to no longer be shocking. As painful as it was to hear about the urban tragedies, the ritual of loss had almost become routine. I could brace myself in light of those circumstances. However, I had never been exposed to a community where children took their own lives. What baffled me more is that there was nothing I could see, from my perspective, that warranted it. It didn't make sense to me and it bothered me so much that I couldn't just teach through the tragedy. I needed to understand what was unspoken. I needed to take a moment to listen. So... I did. I was honest in sharing my concern for the kids' well-being, and my confusion about how so final a choice could be made. I didn't understand what could be so bad when everything they needed was available. Each class shared how they were sometimes made to feel by their peers and parents. They revealed the pressures they faced and the ways they chose to deal with those pressures.

During my last class of the day, I learned that I was the only teacher who paused while teaching to talk to them, and ask about how their feelings. They thanked me...for caring. Their honesty gave me a new set of lenses and helped me gain a deeper understanding of the burdens they carried. It was then that I truly recognized that Black kids didn't have a monopoly on pain. It's just their reactions that are different.

There were absentee fathers in both places. Different reasons for the absence but absent nonetheless. There were children who suffered from trauma in one place while they suffered from depression in another. In both placements there were kids who wanted to go to college yet there were more in the predominantly white school that had no idea why, beyond the belief that it was the logical next step. The majority-minority had external obstacles and physically fought under the guise of respect, reputation or family, while the predominantly white hurt each other through defamation and isolation. In either case, damaged children misplace and misdirect their feelings, and hurt people. No amount of money changed this foolhardy consistency.

Unaware to what extent, I was serving a purpose.

Much like the middle-aged Jewish lady who easily taught a class full of Black and Brown children, here I stood "out of place." I didn't look like them. I wasn't from the community. We seemed to have nothing in common. Yet, they needed me more than I thought that day. Much to my surprise, there were many more days that who I was as their teacher was exactly who I needed to be for them. Via the lessons I taught, connections were made that became lifelong. The experiences I had working with these students helped me tremendously in my own development. Much like in the first half of my career, what lived outside of class time was where I was able to learn so much more about my students. There was an honesty there that allowed all of us to be better.

## LESSON LEARNED: TAKING OWNERSHIP

Teaching in a predominantly white school gave me the chance to grow as an educator. I didn't take anything for granted. The experience allowed me to be intentional about what I taught, and why I taught. I grasped the impact of my role as a medium for students' learning. Although I may have been the first Black male English teacher my students had when I worked in New York, I didn't take ownership of the responsibility; if I had, I could have made useful adjustments to my daily approach to teaching. I was an anomaly in that environment, and needed to leverage that into intentionality. At the predominantly white school, the absence of being surrounded by black children made me more aware and armed me with a strong sense of "otherness." I became relentlessly conscientious. Prior to my new surroundings I didn't accept that everything about me was important. Whether I realized it or not, I was an example to be set, but was not walking in the power of that responsibility. Had I been more aware of myself, who knows what more I could have done in the classroom for the students I served when I first started my career in New York. This was something I had to experience to learn. Now, being in this new space, the necessity of my awareness was important; I recognized that I would be the model for these children. I felt the responsibility to provide dimension to their "possible" perspective of Black men outside of the context of Hip Hop and athleticism. The irony is that I too am Hip Hop. Yet I believed strongly that none of my students would ever be in a position to have intimate interactions with another Black male who might help shape their understanding. I thought of the students as the next generation of people who would employ, marry and work with others who may or may not look like them. I wanted to arm them with an experience with me that would open up their minds rather than default to the comfort of judgment or a stereotypical generalization if gone unchecked. Because of this, I placed Black contributions where they belonged throughout the curriculum, to add breadth of experience beyond my own. After all, Black voices, too, are as American as apple pie and baseball. Through the power of the voices of Hughes, McKay, Douglass, Baldwin, and the trials met through the characters crafted by Hurston and Angelou, we talked of the complexity of social issues. I challenged them to think. I introduced gray. I created the space to have hard conversations where kids could express what they were feeling without being afraid that they would be judged beyond the class. I prefaced the discussions by saying, "I prefer you say ignorant things with me so I can help you before you say them in the world and you get hit on the top of your head for it."

I distinctly remember a student challenging me by asking, "What gives you the right to have these conversations?" My reply was, "I am an educator. If not me, then who else? In what better forum than a classroom?"

As you might imagine, I emphasized these discussions issues and others through literature. We talked about more than just Black issues. We talked about women and their place in America; we talked about the American Dream and what it means for all people, and especially what it meant to these kids as they pursued their own dreams. I learned to marry the text to life while providing them a voice from an educated place. Although they were focused on the grade, the path to their A was going to be aligned to ideas, meaning and analysis. I needed them to do more than regurgitate what they thought I was thinking. In time, they learned that their honest thoughts mattered.

An interesting aspect of working in a predominantly white school was the dynamic of what my presence meant for the few Black students that attended. Of course I did not teach them all (it felt like it) but I found that who I was, and simply being there, was valued more than I'd felt in my previous placement. I felt outwardly appreciated. I could only guess that the Black students that attended the school were feeling the same thing I was hoping to have for myself. The ability to connect with someone that looked like them in a place where they may have felt misunderstood or outside of the dominant culture. This reality shaped the importance of my tenure at this school. I felt the responsibility to uphold a standard of "Blackness" that was exemplary, nuanced and relatable. I placed this on myself and owned it.

The experience helped me realize that all teachers have unique opportunities to represent themselves as models for how children (who would not otherwise come in contact with teachers in any other circumstance) can learn something new about a culture or gender, and gain a level of appreciation that they would not have had otherwise. We as teachers cannot take for granted the uniqueness of our roles as educators. What we each bring to the table matters. Every interaction we have with children is an opportunity. What we do with each opportunity is another matter. Whether the educator realizes it or not, he or she is teaching a child something in each interaction that can mold the student for a very long time. There are many adults today who are in whatever position they are in life thanks to an educator who made them feel good about themselves, and the possibilities associated with who they are and what potential they possess. This is an exponential amount of power that none of us should take lightly. Whether we have been teaching for one day or 40 years, we must always remember the power we possess. We dare not forget. The cost is too great to unconsciously damage the future.

# PART TWO

# REDEFINING MY PURPOSE

# THE NEW GUY

My experiences as a teacher helped me realize why I wanted to go into administration. Thankfully, it was not negatively fueled. I recognized that as a teacher I had a limited yearly reach. For the most part I got the opportunity to teach roughly 140 kids. Add about 20 to 30 more if I chose to sponsor a club. Given what I began to realize about making a difference, I wanted to reach more students. Working with other teachers would increase my reach. If I evaluate 10 to 20 teachers, each has a student load similar to what I once had, or slightly less. Regardless, I can yield more impact through how I support each teacher. Improving the quality and mindset of how one chooses to educate children is invariably positive. My entire focus was about making teachers better for our kids. Sounds pretty good, right!?

Having very little experience beyond the classroom outside of mentorship, some athletic supervision and brief talks with current administrators, I did not have a practical idea of what the daily tasks or the skills of an assistant principal (AP) needed to be to garner successful outcomes. Throughout my experience, there were only a couple of schools that were transparent in how they defined the role of the AP. Some schools had grade-level APs who they functioned as the principal for the grade level. Others had a specific role and only governed over a task. For the most part, it was clear to me that the assistant principal's role was largely defined by what the principal determined.

To ease into the transition and fill the gaps, I applied to take part in an admin leadership training program. My understanding was that it was developed to help those who were not in leadership to learn. To some degree, I was wrong in my assumption that one should be "green." Apparently I was too "green." I wasn't accepted into the program after applying and interviewing two years in a row. After receiving those rejections and feeling "some kinda way," I decided that I would no longer pursue the program. I still wanted to pursue leadership but this wasn't going to be my route. After being asked by the principal if I were going to apply a third time, I shared that I would not but, was open to anything she could provide me if an opportunity arose.

Although she didn't have to, she offered me opportunities: I was given a period to do some low-level discipline that was tied to attendance, supervise athletic events after school and oversee a program to support students who weren't performing. These opportunities gave me some exposure to the big picture of the business of school, and a glimpse into the world of the tasks associated with being an assistant principal. In a small way, I felt like I was doing something. I enjoyed this work. These experiences fueled my desire to be an administrator and dispelled some of my earlier observations about the role. Moreover, the current APs were very receptive to me, and welcomed conversation about what they do. And they let me see a little further too, to help me learn about stress-related details of the position. This reinforced my anticipation of becoming an administrator. At this point in my career I no longer put a limit on where I could lead and support a principal. I recognized that no matter where I went, my focus was on supporting children by way of the adults. The challenge was wide ranging but I had a different mindset about the setting than I did going into education. I was comfortable to lead anywhere.

Fortunately for me there was a shift in positions throughout the county. At the middle school level there was an Instructional Lead Teacher (ILT), who served teachers and took on admin-type duties directly tied to...you guessed it...instruction! This role was going away and was becoming the task of an AP. Consequently, all existing ILTs had to interview for their job under the title of AP. From the outside looking in one would guess that there was a real chance for an AP position all over the county but in reality the person who was the ILT pretty much was going to be the new AP. In my summation of what the district was doing with the position, the interviews for the most part were a formality. If an outside candidate was going to be hired, the sitting principal secretly wanted to replace their ILT and this process would be the safest and less combative way to do so. This was my guess.

So knowing that I really didn't have a snow cone's chance in hell at the position, why did I think this was a good thing? I looked at this in two positive ways: Firstly, this was practice. Secondly, other school administrators would get a chance to meet me. The admin training program was good for those same two reasons: exposure and practice. I received the opportunity to interview for every middle school position that became available. With each interview I made adjustments to my responses, and told myself that I wanted the principal to struggle with the formality of the process. After walking out of the interview like George Jefferson after slamming a door in someone's face, I wanted any and every one to say "Who the hell was *that*?"

By the time I ended the middle school level interviews, an AP position opened up at two of the high schools within the county. I applied to them both. These were real opportunities and after I ran the gauntlet of interviews, administrators knew who I was and could shape clear opinions of my ability to do the job. Prior to this process, no one knew who I was or if I could do the job. Now it was a matter of fit. I had one high school lined up a week apart from the other, and between the first interview and the second, I was offered a position that allowed me to decline the other interview. I couldn't have been happier. I wanted a job and got one. I was receiving the chance to extend my reach.

## THERE IS AN "I" IN TEAM

I walked into the position honestly having no idea what to expect or who I believed I needed to be as an assistant principal. I just wanted to help at another level and do well with what was assigned to me. Because I was green I was open to whatever the job required. The first principal I worked for had a hands-off approach. Everything about Dr. Stephenson made me feel like I was talking to history. This is not my cute way of calling him old. He started out in the system driving a bus and moved up until he sat in this position. He was a part of this community in the way people referred to as *deeply rooted.* He knew where the bodies were buried, the shovels used to complete the job and the owner of the business now housed on top of those nameless bodies. To say the least, I knew he had a lot to offer with respect to what it meant to lead, particularly in this town.

His story was shocking and admirable.

From what I observed, he was the type of leader who trusted the adults to do their job. He understood people and was relationship focused. He had a way of making you feel good no matter the circumstance, and provided some level of wisdom for you to sit with long after the meeting was over. He was a one-of-one leader. What he did only worked for him, and I had nothing less than respect for him. I observed him to be introspective and unassuming. Dr. Stephenson knew more than he showed and mastered the ability to say more by saying less. I admired this quality about him. Who he was helped me shape my understanding of what a principal needed to lead. There was a clear distinction in what the principalship looked like in contrast to the leadership skills I needed as an AP. What he possessed couldn't be taught.

I was among three other APs who had designated roles that were tasks I was most certainly grateful for not having as a new administrator. At the time, I did not have a clearly defined "go to" role, but the position allowed me room to make mistakes without the added weight of how my oversight or inexperience had a school-wide impact. I most certainly wasn't insulated from being judged or from making mistakes, but my decisions had less magnitude than they would later. Being able to handle a "situation" with my colleagues or observe and ask questions allowed me to learn lifelong skills, and avoid putting myself in a hole with teachers because of poor responses to their requests. What was particularly helpful for me was that every one of my colleagues was singular in approach, attitude, demeanor, background, and their relationships with teachers/parents/kids. Disparate in every way except one: we all cared deeply for the kids.

Each of the APs had a distinct personality and presence. Ms. LaGray, whom I affectionately call "The Anvil" was about her business. She played no games in her role, and held everyone accountable. She had roots in the system; her father had been a well-loved administrator but she had earned everything that distinguished her. She had a presence, and during our first meeting she suggested a commitment to hard work.

LaGray was stern and took charge. Meticulous in her responsibilities, she felt that every task needed to be done right. Everyone understood that this was who she was. It was apparent to me that she possessed a history of credibility, and who she was "today" was the result of something and not just a matter of entitlement or just because. If I ever wanted to receive the level of respect she had or walk in the manner she did, I'd need time and stripes. No shortcuts. I appreciated everything that she represented, and although I didn't want to *be* her, I looked forward to working my way up the ladder she stood upon to inhale the air up there.

More importantly, Ms. LaGray took the time to teach me. Whether by being straightforward or by throwing out the phrase, "Before you...you might wanna...." it would be best to just do whatever she suggested. Her "you might wanna" remarks were especially insightful, and nine times out of ten she'd be right. She knew whenever I did the opposite of what she'd suggested, and she never failed afterward to give me a knowing look that said, "See, I was right." No one in admin escaped those "I told you so" moments.

And then there was TJ. An African American man who stood six-foot six, he never met a stranger. Given his size and innate friendliness, staff and students found him impossible to overlook. He personified the phrase, "I know a guy": you would be hard pressed to see him upset. If he was talking, he was either cracking a joke, about to crack a joke or laughing at the person who the joke was about. The kids loved him. They considered him as their Uncle in the sense that he was easy to talk to, take advice from, accept a consequence or ask for a dollar. There was nothing not to like. TJ was the type of person who seemed impervious to criticism; the rare people who spoke ill of him said more about themselves than about TJ. He had a way about handling everyone. He could make a student feel good about receiving a punishment and provide comfort to a parent despite dishing out a suspension. He was able to disarm parents who were upset at the circumstance. The students and parents found refuge in him and connected in such a way that they trusted him. He was a man of the people who could be easily relatable. A lot of who he was I could not be, nor did I need to be. I admired who he was because he helped to dispel an assumption I had had about being an administrator. I did not think you could be unapologetically yourself. Although the Anvil was being true to who she was within the role and outside of it, TJ helped me from the perspective of being a Black male admin. I had assumed that I had to function from a place of defense. I had to be guarded or hold a certain stern demeanor. I need not be too familiar with teachers or students to be taken seriously. These were my initial thoughts. However, TJ added a dynamic I did not possess. He was another Black man in the same position as I. He and I shared a platform and I did not feel burdened to speak or represent all Black males. We could stand next to each other with our own stories, our own approaches, and reach students, parents and teachers in our unique way. Together, we provided a range of complexity that defied the assumptions of people who struggled with "what it means" when a Black male shows up. Thanks to TJ's example, I felt a freedom to own my individuality; the weight of being a symbol or model living in other people's heads was lifted.

Lastly, the Athletic Director, Mr. Pugmire was a pretty carefree type who often reminded me of how much "freedom" we had as admins. When I would ask questions about days off or leaving campus during the day, "just go" and "don't worry about it" were his go-to phrases. He never seemed to have a sense of urgency about the work even when there were instances where he should. There was a messy-ness about him when it came down to following through and getting the job done. He was the type to do three out of the ten steps and hope that the other seven weren't too important. I could sense that how he handled his role did not sit well with TJ, and it infuriated Ms. LaGray. With every interaction between Pugmire and LaGray I could tell that he escaped getting punched in the throat by her only because she knew the cameras were on. As the newbie, I recognized quickly that following Pugmire's lead would not be wise. From him I observed and made note of what not to do.

I was in a uniquely fortunate position. The ability to work with a group that held such a wide range of approaches and perspectives allowed me to quickly recognize the importance of being the best version of myself, rather than looking to fit into a collective archetype. Being the new guy, I wasn't given anything too heavy and was allowed the room to learn and grow. I appreciated the members of the admin team. There was no pressure for me to be like everyone else. Where the expectation existed, though, was in being accountable and to be trusted to do whatever the work required. The bottom line was the answer to the question: "Can I count on you?" The ease by which we could each know that the answer was *yes* when thinking about our colleague is where the strength of the team lived. I felt a sense of belonging.

# TWELVE

If nothing else, within my first year as AP I quickly learned that handling discipline in a timely manner and being present for morning, lunch and dismissal duty was paramount. Being aware and anticipating the possibility for a problem to exist was equally important. I spent a good amount of time watching children and anticipating problems. Initially, I compartmentalized these tasks under the label Keeping Kids Safe. Housed there, I felt less like campus security, but in my heart I knew that this aspect of the job was the one I liked the least. What jumped out at me is that it guaranteed my interactions with children would lead with negativity. My entry point for a conversation centered around correction. I was the embodiment of the handbook, so my presence alone invited tension. This reality was not immediately apparent but I quickly learned that I represented something negative. I had to fight through perception, and the anticipation that I would engage with students combatively. It was important that I was understood in every interaction because I only got one opportunity to make a lasting impression. One. This was the greatest learning curve for me. I was used to having numerous interactions with students, which allowed a relationship to develop. I could have a bad day with a student because I had 179 more chances to erase any negativity and recover from a misstep in judgment or an uncomfortable conversation. Within my role as a teacher, I had many organic reasons to speak to a child. I was a clear resource for a student. As an AP I had to work extremely hard to develop the perspective that I was available as a resource. To the student, my interactions were more from the vantage point of interrogation and inquisition rather than simply to get to know and understand. Consequently, the interactions were often received as disingenuous and veiled, until I disarmed the kids by explaining my purpose for the interaction. I had one chance to demonstrate my value, maintain respect and plant a positive seed. Never before did I think that this type of thinking had to be strongly intentional. Things never seemed to count this much. Well...things always did count for a lot but I never placed this much daily weight on who I was and what I represented. Having lived through the part of the job I liked least, it helped to amplify how I was perceived. Although I didn't like the perception, I could not miss the reality of it. Hence, the reality of it helped me to work toward doing something about it; the ends justified the means. Time afforded me the introspection but prior to it... I hated hall duty.

Although it was our responsibility to provide support and safety, hall duty felt the least like the role of an educator. I felt mostly like law enforcement. I was there to look for trouble—to remind students of rules they are breaking and to interact to correct behavior, clear the halls, keep crowds from forming and usher kids to class. If I could receive ten cents for every time I had to say "take your hood off please" I would be a rich man. If I had another ten to determine if someone was violating the dress code, I would be on the Forbes Wealthiest list. I often told myself I didn't sign up for this, then quickly realized...yes, I did.

Outside of these interactions (which I found to be a gateway for students to get into *more* trouble based upon their response to a request), I was available to be called to address what we unaffectionately called "a situation." Just so we are all on the same page, "a situation" ranged from a minor negative interaction that we were called by the teacher to handle, to an issue involving multiple students, which could have two of us tied up for a large part of the day. Whenever called to "a situation," I quickly learned what support looked like in the eyes of a teacher. Having lived through quite a few, this is how they played out:

- Prior to my arrival, Mr. or Ms. Teacher had a negative exchange with a student.
- The student said something that the teacher felt was disrespectful.
- Mr. or Ms. Teacher warned/threatened that they were going to call an administrator if the student didn't stop the disruptive behavior and comply with Teacher's instructions.
- Student doesn't stop, or simply says "So... call them" (insert whatever tone you like).
- Outraged by the insubordination, Teacher has no choice but to call.
- Entire class stops and waits for an administrator to

arrive.

- Until we arrive, Teacher chooses to continue to antagonize the student, or speak to consequences they are not in control of.
- Student and Teacher become increasingly upset
- I or we...ARRIVE

My administrative colleagues and I were often called to classrooms with the expectation to publicly support any affront that might take place in our presence. No matter the circumstance, in the heat of the moment I was there to be a teacher's backup. They were mad so I had to show some level of stern indignation when I arrived. I was there to receive a verbal recount of the negative interaction encountered before my arrival—while I now stood in the doorway of the classroom in front of the student and the entire class. Teacher often pointed and loudly explained the complaint, while the student (ignoring Teacher's demand for silence) tried to verbalize his or her own side of the story. Teacher finished with, "I don't want him in my class!" or "I need her to leave!" And I, who had no intention ever to have an argument in front of the class or a dispute about who was right or wrong, would simply say, "Come with me." My deadliest response: "Get your things" (insert stern tone and emotionless face).

To clarify, I understood that one of my primary responsibilities was to ensure a positive learning environment. To help students feel safe in a space to learn, free of distraction, is a part of the job. Teachers having the right to teach and feel safe is a part of the job. I had to play a role in ensuring that this could happen. What I disliked had everything to do with how teachers made me feel when it came to supporting them with discipline, and how students viewed why I was there.

I was being "sicced on" children.

My presence automatically escalated the situation. And whatever issue started before I arrived automatically became my problem. I was being placed in an adversarial scenario whether I wanted to be or not. Moreover, I did not like how I was spoken to. I felt fetched to be "the heavy," no matter the circumstance. During the pivotal moment of each interaction, I felt professionally inferior to the teacher. It sounds odd or even funny, but the reality is that in these situations, teachers talked down to me. They were not requesting my help to solve a problem—they were demanding that I do *what they say*. They weren't calling me because of my artful negotiation and understanding of children. They were calling me to remove the student. If they could remove the student on their own, I would probably never receive the call. In their eyes *this* was my job. This was the consensus, and I could not accept that that defined my value. I struggled to understand how teachers arrived at this definition of the assistant principal's sole role and responsibility, but everything in me was destined to change it. I had to. Either I change it or re-evaluate my decision to enter leadership. This did not feel good.

Fast forward to the conversation in my office.

Having realized that I only get one chance with every student, I tried to make the most of my interaction, even though I was handling discipline. I used my time to understand. I allowed the student to share what he or she believed happened. I wanted their perspective. I genuinely wanted to know, and reserved judgment until I heard the student completely. I did not want the consequence to be a foregone conclusion. I sincerely wanted them to have a voice. So I listened and asked questions to get the entire story. Afterward, I usually would identify the truth as lying somewhere in the middle. Following that, I'd determine the consequence. It was important to me to find the "point of responsibility" for the student. Even when the circumstance may have revealed that it was more of an adult behavior that caused a scenario to escalate, I wanted to make sure that the student always understood their part in it. The "it" was where I could focus on choices and help the student to see why their response to what they perceived to be disrespectful is where they made the mistake. There was nothing more dangerous to me than how a student responds when they believe they are right and whatever is happening to them is "not fair." There is an immaturity that blinds them, with emotion is at the forefront. The frustration builds, and their awareness of a foregone outcome that will not end in their favor amplifies the response. The mere presence of an administrator or, God forbid, the School Resource Officer can quickly turn an upset student who may just need a conversation into a screaming and unhinged kid who has managed to turn a dress code violation into a five-day suspension.

Having seen this play out many times, I wanted students to understand that there was a legitimate route to a different outcome, one that keeps their dignity intact and their voices heard. It was important to me not to invalidate how they were made to feel. I was sure to highlight that it was okay for them to be upset, but that they could learn how to navigate through their anger to properly address the teacher behavior that caused them to react badly. I emphasized the fact that timing is key. The time to argue about being right was never going to work in the student's favor with an audience of his or her peers, at the teacher's expense. The teacher will respond to gain control of the class in whatever way that seems fit. However, by waiting until after class or another day beyond the moment to share how what the teacher said or did made you feel, the teacher will hear your concern. He or she will be more likely to take it seriously and make an adjustment so the miscommunication doesn't happen again. Maturity and professionalism should prevail.

It was in these exchanges that I felt better about being the disciplinarian. My goal was not about discipline. I focused on consequences attached to choices, and a teachable moment that would allow room for a better choice down the road. Was every instance received well? No. In some instances...*Helllllll no.* The student was either too upset or had no desire to join me in my moment of restorative practices. In those instances, it was my job to learn not to take it personally and remain objective. I was not the enemy. Yet, it hurt me to know that for some, I most certainly was. In the eyes of some, including parents, my role was to dole out consequences "over nothing" or "for nothing." I was the embodiment of the execution of a teacher's "or else..." and *this* was not what I signed up for.

Despite my attempt to support the students I encountered when I engaged them for discipline, it wasn't enough to change the perception of my role. I made a conscious choice to engage with students without them being in trouble, to shift how they saw me. What I found interesting was if I spoke to a student while at lunch, or engaged a student in the hall or the library or anywhere, there was an automatic fear that I was speaking to them because they did something wrong. They wouldn't want to engage in a conversation with me because my presence suggested to their peers that they *did* do something wrong. I had to work at changing this negative feeling based upon my presence alone. As someone who did not come off as warm and fuzzy, I understood the barriers I created for myself. I couldn't duplicate the finessed approach of my colleague, TJ. I couldn't make them comfortable in the manner that he could. They weren't just going to walk up to me and start talking. I wasn't as inviting. I suffer from what some may call resting bitch face (RBF): a resting scowl. Imagine your driver's license picture on your face all day. That's me. Unintentionally, I am not inviting. You're not getting teeth from me. Well...not right away. I recognize I have a wall up and it's a thing I am working on but it has no reflection on who I am or how I really feel. To push away is never my intention. I had to find my way to connect with students as an administrator.

The last thing I wanted to do was make things uncomfortable in the name of trying to build relationships. Over time, those genuine moments presented themselves. I began to earn a level of comfort among students that made sense for me. I didn't have to be anything more than who I am. The credibility developed. My expectations were clear but I was fair and continued to show students and parents that I cared. This credibility allowed room for me to work more closely with students through mentorship. Having been there long enough to understand the needs and where opportunities lived, I wanted to do my part.

What is important to note is that this growth happened after my first year as an administrator, and when a new principal came to the school. Dr. Tyler came from another school in the system, and had been a colleague of mine there. He knew what he wanted to achieve in his new placement. Fortunately, our relationship allowed for me to embark on this initiative to establish a formal mentorship program. He supported what I wanted to do and felt that our students would benefit from my leadership in this way. Every principal has a unique perception of what an assistant principal should do, and how they should function to support the school community. It was not lost on me that I could have been told "no." He could have easily shared data that placed an emphasis somewhere else rather than on what I believed was important. My initiative could easily have been pushed to the side or shelved indefinitely. The manner in which I was supported by him in this moment and beyond as an assistant principal helped in my development as a principal, and reinforced how I saw the roles of the assistant principals who would eventually work with me. Dr. Tyler was able to recognize the passion I had for children, along with my unique ability to add value and allow who I was to be what was needed without having to make it about him for it to happen.

I decided to duplicate a mentorship similar to the one in New York. A friend and frat brother who still resided in that state helped me revamp what this program should be, and move it forward. It was called Shaping Him into Future Talent (SHIFT). With this program I saw an opportunity to support the young men at the school beyond the classroom, while sparking their entrepreneurial spirit. I requested referrals from teachers and the school counselors for potential students. I called each of the students from class and explained what the program was supposed to be to gauge their interest. I moved forward with a parent meeting and got started. The program allowed me to have a new interaction with students that was disarming. I found the organic space to communicate. More importantly, I gave the students a different lens by which to judge me.

I worked with young men to be proactive in relationship building while creating opportunities for them to belong to something that was positive. What was started and accomplished through the program cemented my intention, and revealed my willingness to do more than what was in my job description. This is where I made my mark as an administrator. When I was beginning to feel low and heavy about the work, I created a lane to hunker down in that provided a meaningful balance to tasks that I did not feel represented my purpose. By developing a means to connect with children, I saved my dampened spirit. Where negativity had once dominated my thoughts, I now chose to focus on the good I could do simply by being present. Although in an authoritative role, I found balance between the tasks I managed, the support I was providing for teachers, and doing whatever was in my power to help children. The person I was shaping myself into allowed me to feel valued and necessary.

I expected future hiccups associated with the job, but I didn't feel that those moments would outweigh what I was there to do. By no means was it perfect but, having been able to serve in a majority-minority school that was unlike anything I experienced before, it provided a new lens for me. Where I'd once held a sadness about the trajectory for students of color at a public school, I now felt promise.

## QUICK ASIDE: THE BAGGAGE

As a Black man in education, I'm often cast in a role as the "answer" to control Black boys. Whether it be through the title of dean, assistant principal or principal, we are seen foremost through the lens of disciplinarian. Whenever a school is considered to be out of control, the best fit is a Black man. Otherwise, we serve in the capacity of a coach or mentor whose purpose is to save Black boys. The box we are placed in as the disciplinarian reinforces a negative perception of why we exist in schools. Whether directly or indirectly, the manner in which we are placed in a position of authority reinforces the idea of policing Black children and supporting the school-to- prison pipeline. If you think I'm being hyperbolic, consider this. Think about all the Black men that ever crossed your path in education. What was their role? What do you remember? How many were coaches? Deans? Assistant Principals? Principals? What stands out most? No matter your experience, the truth of the matter is Black men are one of the least represented subgroups in education. The scarcity of Black men in education amplifies our interaction and actions within education. The baggage associated with this underrepresentation made me feel that I had to represent more than just who I am and who my parents raised me to be. I felt judged against the stereotype of Black men at large. I felt examined, and because of this I entered all spaces in education working through assumptions and being careful not to replicate or support generalizations about Black men. Every interaction had the potential to support or counteract the perception of who we are as educators, and who we are outside of education We are always teaching others about who Black men are, in ways verbal and nonverbal—whether we want to or not, whether we are equipped to or not.

I carry that sensitivity because I can feel myself swallow my instinct whole in response to colleagues, or those whom I evaluate, or parent—all to make sure that I am "approachable" and not "aggressive." Show teeth (still working on this). Relax my eyebrows. Pay attention to nonverbal posture. Am I being too forward? Watch your tone. Measure each word. Make eye contact and smile. Speak with warmth. Pull back. In my interactions as an assistant principal, I carried these thoughts into every scenario. My greatest struggle during the transition in this role had everything to do with perception. I was fortunate to have had another Black male in administration. His presence allowed room for me to exist more within my skin than to be everything for every Black boy. Yet, who I am, and was *perceived to be*, presented me with the *responsibility to be* the model. To mentor. To save. To father. To uncle. There was an incessant need that I had to willingly accept, despite the reality that I could give my all but I could not be everything these Black boys needed.

In the eyes of others, the meaning of my "everything" varies wildly from situation to situation, and from setting to setting. Even before I open my mouth, my presence alone causes disruption and assumption. Whether I like it or not.

## LESSON LEARNED: THE COST OF EMPOWERMENT

As assistant principals, we serve to implement the vision of the principal. In many regards we are taskmasters and managers who do our best to execute the tasks at hand. We know we've done a good job only in the silence and absence of criticism after the execution of the task we were given. An excellent AP makes what he or she does seem optically easy and insignificant. We are gatekeepers and filters. However, the position can be much more if the principal allows it to be.

Having been an assistant principal in two different settings, I was able to quickly ascertain how assistant principals can feel empowered and be a part of the solutions needed to move a school community forward--or feel insignificant, devalued and limited to utilize their strengths for the good of the school community. Whichever way the situations turn out for assistant principals, the outcomes are driven by perspective, educational philosophy and, in some cases, ego.

On one hand, a principal can establish that the buck stops at his or her desk, but with that perspective, the principal may not be willing to take certain risks, or allow the assistant principal to do something that he or she feels uncomfortable doing. Why? Because of how the action's poor execution or failure may reflect on the principal rather than focus on the intention of the idea, the assistant principal's talents, leadership and gifts to execute the idea, and its impact on children. The limitations and fears that live in the mind of the principal can potentially stifle the assistant principal's professional progress.

Then there is the philosophy of the principal that has an

impact on the assistant principal's role. If the principal believes that the role of the assistant principal exists only within the task assigned, then the scope and growth of the AP is limited and/or diminished. By default, he or she can be devalued by staff members simply because of the task that is assigned for the AP to manage. The assistant principal can become the one who deals with...and has no expertise on...for the duration of their appointment.

Lastly, there is ego. Some principals believe that if the blame is placed at the doorstep of the principal's office then the glory should also be hung above the principal's door. Any idea or initiative that is approved by the principal should become the principal's idea; and if it is the principal's idea, then the principal must be involved in the minutiae of the process. There should be checkpoints of approval for everything. Otherwise, nothing good can happen for the school unless it comes out of the principal's office. Consequently, this mindset does not give an AP any room to choose to contribute or be innovative or make any suggestions for improvement because they already understand that he or she will not be heard. Therefore, in lieu of making decisions and learning how to lead, he or she can only move under the approved steps and watchful eye of their Queen or King Ruler Almighty.

The pitfalls that exist in each of these characteristics of a principal are very real. Shared leadership is not a silver bullet that guarantees effective leadership. However, there is value in understanding the strengths of your APs and supporting them to develop so that they can become effective leaders in their own rights.

This cannot be done without proper practice, preparation and resources. As a teacher and later as an AP, I had the privilege of observing many leaders. I developed as a leader because I paid attention to the action of each and asked questions to better understand the decisions that were being made. During the time I served as an AP, I initially felt diminished because my purpose was not defined beyond the task of discipline. I felt like the police (better known by the kids as 12) because I was not defined in any other capacity to support teachers or work with students outside of that task. I do not feel that my first principal had any other intention besides the philosophy that APs existed to support the teachers and allow them to teach. If that meant removing students from school all day, then that was what would be important. When under the leadership of a different principal at a majority white school, I felt like I was there for decoration. I had a limited scope of value and was not asked to contribute other than for the sake of saying that "Everyone had a chance to share." I felt like I was wasting away. I was not trusted to do discipline or execute the tasks that I was given without prior approval and constant check-ins. Anything that I decided to do out of the interest of what I thought was best was not supported. I was made to feel insignificant, and I did.

However, when being led by someone who believed I brought some value, Dr. Tyler empowered me within my expertise and coached me in the areas of my weakness. I felt empowered to perform, and began to acquire my voice as a leader. My ideas were not met with opposition. They were met with probing questions that allowed me to think through some things that I may not have considered before moving forward. He would lead with, "This is what I'd like to do ... tell me why it won't work." Then we talked through it together until the idea became more practical and crystalized. It became our work and our idea.

How I was made to feel as an assistant principal has a lasting impact on how I support the assistant principals with whom I work. Ms. Ford and Ms. Milligan are two of the most intelligent women I ever met. They have unique strengths that I do not possess. I need them. We need each other. They are level 5 leaders whose first considerations are students, and how our actions reflect on the school. I never witnessed a decision that was made because of the way Ms. Ford believed it would work to her professional benefit. There was no decision made by Ms. Milligan that she intended to be acknowledged as "a Milligan decision" that benefited the school. Both women serve the school and place their own needs last. They lead from a place of "how we can help," and live in the mantra of "whatever it takes." Because of their care, innovation and love, we move forward. Because I place value in who they are and move out of their way, we all move forward. Because of what I learned and lived through, I made a decision to empower others.

# PART THREE

# THE NECESSITY OF BEING NECESSARY

# THE GREATEST AWARD

On the night of my appointment to the principalship I, along with other appointees, was asked to come to the board meeting. Nervous. Excited. Those words best describe how I was feeling. I scanned the room to see familiar faces who smiled and mouthed congratulations. The words met me at the eyes but I could feel it all over. I was happy. I showed all of my teeth (finally!). Among the people present was a woman I was particularly gratified to greet. Jade had been the first principal of the school that I now would lead. There was a buffer between her tenure and my appointment so I wasn't walking into her immediate footsteps. However, the imprint of her legacy was something I believed I needed to aspire to. There are many words to describe her from those who encountered her or had worked with her, and none suggested anything less than pure professionalism. When I looked at her I thought of the way I wanted others to speak of my leadership; I hoped to be one of those storied leaders that other admins talk about with admiration, because of the principal's character, and the way that *that* particular leader made students, staff and the community feel. She was my ghost to chase, in the manner that Kobe regarded Jordan. She had no idea.... until now. During this moment of "coronation," we greeted each other. As we hugged in celebration of my appointment, it was if my thoughts were posted somewhere on my forehead. No sooner than she pulled me in that she spoke in my ear: "They have never had a Marcus Broadhead. You are going to be fine."

This statement said so much to me. On the one hand, I reflected back on my interview for the principalship. I distinctly remember saying that I wanted to be as close to who I am as possible. I rejected the idea of not being myself by putting on a veil that I could not live up to beyond the interview. I wanted the panel to know who I was, and to make its decision based upon me. If hired, I did not want to have to live up to anything other than who I am. I remember leaving the interview feeling good. I represented myself well and had no regrets. It was a situation where I was able to say, if I am chosen for this position then who I am is what they want. If I do not get the position, then who I am is *not* what is needed, so *good*, this job is *not* right for me. My frame of mind completely removed the regrets that one normally feels following an interview. You know: that feeling when you review all your answers and curse at some of the responses you gave. I didn't feel any of that. I was at peace.

On the other hand, Jade's words fueled me to lead by making the best decisions that I believed needed to be made. It was not going to be about what others before me had done, or what another leader does at his or her school. It was going to be about doing the right thing for kids and working toward creating a place that gave the right foundation for life beyond the school. I could avert the ghost. To make decisions without second guessing myself was freeing. I was not chained by the question: What would Jade do?

I thought of my childhood experience in middle school, and began to think through the challenges I'd faced as a student. I thought of my experience as a teacher at a middle school and what I believed to be important, and then I thought of my experience as an assistant principal and asked, "What did I tell myself that I wanted to do if I ever had the chance to make the decisions?" All of those thoughts brought me to the point where I was now. I was in a position to choose a road map of implementation. The ghosts I chose to chase were rooted in the leader I wanted for myself.

## THE STORY I TOLD MYSELF

Before I go further, I am going to take some liberties when using the pronoun "we." I know that I speak for myself. Yet when walking into the position at this juncture in my life, I wholeheartedly believed that I was a part of a collective that shared similar ideas about the choice to be an educator, and the mission associated with the career. As much as I would like to vouch for them all, I do not know all Black men. I know that we all have different journeys, paths and rationales that bring us to education, to teach or counsel and to pursue administration. The oneness in "we" was at the center of the boulder-sized chip on my shoulder that I held with one arm in the same posture as an 80s b boy with a JVC radio. I was a part of something bigger that was necessary for the transformation, so at this point, I didn't feel as if what was about to take place was singular. This was *me* doing my part for *us*.

For the few (percentage-wise) Black men who enter education, *if* we make it past those first three to five years, some move into administration. In light of the scarcity coupled with one's perceived ability, most Black male administrators are most often appointed to turnaround schools, or majority-minority schools. For argument's sake, I am referring to post-desegregation—to whatever point in time that you are reading this book. Moreover, if appointed to a principalship, we are placed at failing majority-minority schools. We come to these schools feeling an urgency *to combat familiar issues* (vividly represented in the early part of the movie *Lean On Me*). Violence. Chaos. Failure. Apathy. A lack of everything present in schools with foundations for success. We are given the keys to troubled schools as a last-ditch effort to allow us to take care of our own. The expectation is that the Black male leader will "transform the school," which usually means that the Black male leader will provide order and discipline under the guise of improving culture and climate. I call it the Daddy's-home design for creating a culture of success. Leading by might and fear

In this environment, variables outside the locus of the principal's control negatively affect the school. The principal must be mindful of this, and have a plan to even have hope for what can be controlled in the building. In most cases, Black male principals who want children to learn have to figure out how to solve poverty, disenfranchisement, and systemic racism from the seat of the principalship. To say the least, this is a tall order. Despite the insurmountable nature of the task, we seek out schools that resemble the ills afflicting the community because we believe that the principalship is a position best pursued in places where Black men are needed most. We can be made to feel that to serve in any other environment makes us guilty of professional and cultural failure. Majority-minority schools have a connection and familiarity that allows us to feel like a part of the solution. We were raised to believe that education is a pathway to something better, and for the most part, this concept has worked for us. Because we come back to our communities to provide opportunities for our people, we are models of success.

Heroism mixed with survivor's guilt is the great elixir we pour into our daily coffee. It is the fuel by which we define our success or our failures. In the back of our minds (but at the forefront of our conscience) we ask ourselves: What will be enough? Am I enough? What happens if I fail them? Whether I wanted to or not, I could not shake this sense of duty.

Compounding my obligation to duty, I was the product of a broken system. This is something I'm keenly aware of. How I was taught—or should I say, *prepared* for life beyond high school I will never forget. For me, wanting more was a singular motivation. A culture of negativity was what ran the school, and those that did not subscribe to the negativity, who wanted more for themselves, had to find it on their own. The expectations for students were minimal. Either you graduated or failed out. There was no structure to push for anything more nuanced and complex. The school motto should have been, "Are you finished or are you done?" Either way, administrators wanted you gone. This was a systemic failure that I absorbed as truth. I wondered why this had to be *our* story and not an outlier.

My personal circumstance shaped me to believe that a majority-minority school was synonymous with violence and failure. I knew of no public school with a majority of Black children and other students of color that flourished. During the time that I was growing up there were more Eastside Highs and not a Morgan Freeman, Michelle Pfeiffer or Edward James Olmos in sight.

Will this school be another failing Black one under the leadership of another Black man? If it is broken, what power do I have to effect systematic change? Do I have the stamina to lead? Would what I know to be effective elsewhere work inside a majority-minority school?

Add this to my list of Other Duties and Responsibilities.

Lastly, my experience as a teacher in majority-minority schools under the leadership of Black men gave me insight into how they led. I was fortunate enough to be close enough to each to pick their brains about their roles, and the variety of situations they faced. Mr. Ray was my former math teacher, so I had a long-term investment in how I viewed him and his leadership. Having just begun in the profession, I wanted to learn from him, and felt comfortable being in a building where my former teacher was now the principal. Initially, I was proud of him and excited to work at the school. At times I took the liberty to meet with him to ask questions, or just to get an idea of what his day was like.

Mr. Lee was someone I initially identified with and admired because he was the first principal I'd encountered who made the idea of being a principal look like a cool thing. He dressed fashionably well. He drove a Mercedes-Benz. Lee didn't appear to be much older than I was, yet he was in the highest position that that building offered. He appeared untraditional, and made the idea of being a principal something attainable. I learned a lot from these men but not for the reasons one might expect. From both I learned what not to do, or to be clearer, what I won't do.

Although each had very different styles at the core of who they were, I could not appreciate their choices and approach to leadership. I observed that their choices were self-serving, and less about real leadership, which was contrary to who I was and what I thought the principalship was about. To say the least, I was highly disappointed. In hindsight, I placed on them the responsibility to teach me how to lead. Neither was prepared to do that, and if they'd been aware of my expectations, they probably wouldn't have cared to fill the role. Yet they taught me more than they could ever conceive. My observation of them taught me not to allow a title to define my character; rather, the title must serve as a reminder of my responsibility that my title holds. They were Black men, and who they were and how they handled the responsibility of the role sat upon my shoulder as a reminder to anyone who would, unbeknownst to me, choose my actions as a measuring stick for their own ceiling of expectations.

All of this was what I was carrying.

# INTRODUCING DR. BROADHEAD

I made a choice to start with who I am. Having recognized that judgment comes from ignorance, I did not want to put myself in a position where the mystery of who I am would overshadow the reality of who I am. I chose to be as transparent as I could be from the onset. I wanted my faculty to know that I was an English teacher who taught for 12 years, and that the challenges and failings I saw at eye level helped shape me into a better educator. I wanted them to know that making it here was always about who I grew into as a teacher first, and further, that I'll always consider myself to be a teacher. I wanted them to know how I was taught, and to what degree these experiences fed into my hopes for the school and the work that was in front of us. I wanted them to know that I understood the challenge we faced as a school that recently merged faculties and received a demographic of students that the school traditionally didn't house. With one fell swoop of redistricting, the student body went from roughly 500 students who were academically, economically and culturally homogeneous to 1000 students who reflected a diversity of strengths and challenges. Although I recognized tension in the building, I felt that where we were going was more important than where we had been. Whether it was said during my initial faculty meeting as an introduction, in small groups or in one-on-one meetings, I shared this Song of Myself often.

I wanted the community to know what I cared about and what I envisioned for the school. I acknowledged their concerns but I also shared the importance of their support along the way. I met with any parent or group that wanted to meet with me to share their concerns about their experiences at the school. I did a lot of listening and learned quite a bit about the community's concerns. My first year brought a truly awesome feeling. I felt supported and lifted up by the community. Some parents told me directly that they did not want to see me fail. I could not ask for more from them. I was honored.

What I've failed to share until this point is that my approach to my first year was not developed in a vacuum. The school and community had a history that helped me understand that I needed take some small, intimate steps before I could begin to look at academics. There was a herd of elephants in the room, each one standing on its hind legs and singing show tunes. I had to decide which issues to address first. I understood that the things I could control had to be where I started. I had to gain the community's trust and respect, while building my credibility among my staff. I considered the decisions I needed to take on the front end to start the process, and get small wins.

What I had going for me was that I was not a stranger. The community had seen me interact with their children as an assistant principal of the local high school. The staff knew me as someone who came down to work with teachers to prepare them for their rising 9th graders. I was also fortunate to have taught some of the teachers' children. They knew me as their peer and understood how I cared for their children. There was never a clearer example of the statement, "Be careful of how you treat the people on the way up...."

But despite feeling some level of familiarity and comfort to start the change that I wanted to see, I could not take any previous relationship for granted. I worked to be strategic about where I hoped to take the school. I created a four-phase plan that outlined the focus of each phase. I considered my own experience of middle school and thought, "How can I make middle school memorable for the right reasons?" I recalled the few years that I taught at that level, and considered what could be put in place to allow the space for teachers to grow. And then I recalled my time at an "effective school," and pondered how to achieve helpful and consistent parent commitment. How can I mobilize parents to positively affect the school's culture and climate? These were my big questions.

My questions aside, the school was bent beneath a reality that I could not ignore.

The staff went through an abrupt shift in leadership. Not long before the shift, the school experienced a demographic shift due to redistricting. The school literally became a Title I school with varied needs overnight. The ramification of the redistricting was a sore spot for the entire community. In the aftermath, the faculty between the two schools merged, and most parents who had students at the school prior to redistricting requested special permission to pull out their children. Some sold their homes and moved to parts of town where their children could attend another school. The affected school's new principal was not from either community. An assistant principal from each of the schools, who were brought together, held the same roles. Consequently, there was a learning curve that did not allow both assistant principals to operate from their strengths. The transition did not go too well. The greatest issue was a lack of a unified vision and approach that would help to establish a new school culture. Tension existed among staff and administration, and a lack of professional cohesiveness modeled the wrong set of behaviors for the children. The community mistrusted school leadership, and parents felt that their children were not being treated fairly. Concerns about racism were rumbling. For everyone involved, this was not a positive period.

Furthermore, there was trauma from this experience that no one addressed. As the new leader, I recognized that I was up against the habits and expectations of the leadership that preceded me. The norms that had been established could run up against my leadership. If it had been the educators' experience that leadership doesn't want to hear from staff, and that teachers' ideas and opinions can live only on an annual survey, there would be much more work for me to do, to break this belief and receive honest input throughout the year. A staff member who believes that he or she is not valued by the administration is a real challenge, and one of the most difficult transformational third order changes to sustain. Because every staff member has a unique perspective, navigating their "educational PTSD" takes time. A principal must note the individual's pain point and then work toward building credibility that reshapes the negative generalization that "all admins...", and attributes positives and/or negatives directly to our interaction. With this in mind I had to be mindful and kept the question: What action could I take that would not trigger the pain point?

Given my understanding of the school's history, my focus was going to be character based. Everyone needed direction but they needed to feel good about being guided, and about following. My approach borrowed from my approach to teaching. It was all about relationship building. I needed to understand who was working in the building as much as they needed to understand who *I* was. Over time, we could build a professional relationship that was meaningfully deeper than the surface pleasantries. I spent a month meeting with every staff member to get a sense of who they are and what they thought was important for the school as well as for themselves. I didn't expect to have a deep psychological moment but I wanted everyone to have a moment to talk. From these moments, I found genuine entry points to follow up on throughout the year. On the other hand, my daughter attended the school with me as a 6th grader which gave interested staff a chance to see me in my role as a father. The opportunity to view me beyond the position I held had a nuancing effect that gave my presence some added depth and humanity. I became something more than what some teachers had initially thought. At the time, I just wanted my daughter to be close to me; it was a naturally hectic time in her life, and I wanted to be honest about her experiences, particularly as they related to what other children at the school were experiencing.

This way, I gave students, too, an easy opening to see me.

To allow for communication points, I chose to be actively visible. Walking the halls every morning and speaking to staff was a way to check their pulse, see who was present, and allow them to quickly get my perspective on something that didn't require a formal meeting. It was during those morning walks that I saw who was having a moment, or who was starting the day with the right attitude and energy for our kids. I was also available to talk and check in with them during their stints on lunch duty. I wanted them to count on me being in those two places if they had something they wanted to share.

I regard my staff members not just as my colleagues, but as my students. I have to know them. They have to know me. I have to find a way to connect. I need them to be comfortable. From my experiences with the principals I had as a teacher, I didn't feel comfortable approaching them, and when I did, the interaction felt like an event. I remembered feeling as kid that, if I ever had an interaction with the principal, the meeting would be a one-time event related to something extraordinarily good or really bad. I would've remembered it my whole life.

## AS CLEAR AS MUD

I wanted communication to be two-way. I wanted to open up dialogue that would help me understand where we were as a school—not in opinion but in reality. I didn't want two versions of what happened at the school: what I thought versus what was really happening. Communication was the only way that I would truly know anything beyond what I was able to observe. With this in mind, I established a structure of informal and formal communication. I felt pretty comfortable with the system that was in place to allow teachers to have a voice. I didn't want anyone to feel that only certain people were able to talk with me, or that some staffers might be denied access and a voice. This wasn't going to be my version of *The Wiz*. Every perspective mattered to me. You didn't need to hold a specific title or attend a special leadership meeting to be heard. No formal agenda required.

Formal conversations were established through different meetings that ranged from grade level to whole school. I needed a year of those meetings before I decided to do anything differently than before. I wasn't a fan of meeting to meet out of habit. Time is important, and I wanted what was to be discussed to have value and purpose. It was important to me to be honest about what can be done or can't. I never wanted to entertain a conversation about something that I already had made my mind up about. Let me clarify: I make educated decisions. The education comes from listening to those closest to the work, or to objective experts. I am open to dialogue at the beginning of decision making. I need to understand. I am open to revisiting a decision that was made every 30 days after living with it so we can make adjustments.

Every one of my decisions has a 30-day shelf life for me. Let's commit for 30 so we can honestly reflect and adjust. If ,upon our review on the 31st day, I find that there was a gap in the commitment, we can't do more than recommit, to have a true understanding of the expected outcome. If I have made the decision, my approach for discussion centers on what can go wrong with what I have proposed. That way, we can take the time to address those hiccups and find solutions. My lead is always, "I plan to do this...tell me why I shouldn't... Are these obstacles truly cataclysmic or merely rooted in our own discomfort about the overall goal?

I had developed methods of communication, and followed them, but then I began to run up against something I'd never counted on: avoidance. Those who were guilty may call it something else, but that's what I called it. I had numerous information-gathering meetings and healthy discussions about choices that make the most sense. The responses I received made me comfortable that we had a consensus to move forward. And then I'd discover that there were issues or concerns that we hadn't discussed. I would hold another meeting to get to the bottom of this concern, and get a feeling of resolution—only to find out a day or two later that there were still things that were left unsaid, and that had an impact on the decisions we were making. The behavior also reared its head when a staff member expressed frustration with another staff member's work ethic, teaching style, meeting etiquette or whatever, and then complain to everyone about the behavior. And although the complainers would ask to not be placed on the team, they would not ever talk to the person about the behavior. I could not understand for the life of me why there was an avoidance to be direct or to speak up, especially when the situation had a direct impact on the complainer

I remember having a *New Jack City* Nino Brown moment during a faculty meeting called to drive home the point that I could not function with dishonesty. I took pride in being transparent, even to a fault. However, I expected the same from my staff. In a moment of visual metaphor, I showed the group a video of a trick being played on someone. Everyone but the victim was in on the joke. When the video ended I said that I was the person being tricked, and they were the ones that were in on the culture of not being truthful, out of some level of fear. I explained that as a New Yorker, we stab you in the front. I went on to express my frustration with their approach to communication. I was exhausted by the behavior and could not continue to have meeting after meeting just because those I needed to trust were unwilling or not ready to tell the truth, no matter how it was going to make all of us feel. Did I offend? Yup! During that time, though, I saw no other way than to be brutally direct about what I saw happening. The consequences of unacceptable behavior were immense, so I was ready to die on this hill.

This was a huge hurdle for me because I didn't understand the logic. I was putting in the work. I established communication. However, what I didn't take into account was time and personnel. Was what I was asking of them coming too soon for them to accept? Had I taken into account that what I expected had never been expected of them before? I didn't consider that this change was bigger for them than for me. I hadn't recognized that although I was being transparent, I was giving them too much to absorb. They needed more time to digest my expectations, and I didn't give them the space to grow into what I needed them to be. I saw a group of mature women and assumed that the respect I had for their experience would be welcomed. I wanted my requests to be perceived as refreshing rather than burdensome, and for the staff to see me as the principal they'd been hoping for.

What I didn't know was that my way of addressing issues made most of the staff uncomfortable. Why? Because for them, any level of confrontation was synonymous with combative tension. I wanted clarity of communication, and an environment in which all of us could speak to concerns and find solutions. To some degree it was premature.

I dug a bit deeper to reflect, and understand that even given my good intentions, my communication had to be an exact science. What was my body language conveying? What was I saying when I didn't say a word? When I did speak, how was my tone? I even considered the possibility that there was a significant "new" happening for them, too. With a predominantly white staff, when did they ever have to engage daily with a Black man? In what capacity? More importantly, have they ever had to answer to a Black man before? Did my physical presence intimidate them? And if it did, were my words being misconstrued?? It bothered me that I even had to think such a thing. However, it forced me to be mindful of every aspect of my communication. When will it be appropriate for me to raise my voice? Never. I would have to carefully think before I spoke. Filter. Do not be demonstrative. What might my actions communicate to the observer across the cafeteria? When is it reasonable to be obviously upset or disappointed? What does communicating these feelings look like? Can I ever communicate these feelings?

These questions were ones I had to run through in just a few seconds before giving any response during interactions with staff. To temper my angst, I sought counsel from my pastor, who gave me advice that changed my entire perspective on working with my staff. The advice was this: think more about how you're treating them than about how you're leading them. After I expressed my frustrations, fears and "hope-fors," the pastor asked me if I'd read a book by Gary Chapman, *The Five Love Languages.* I was pleased to respond that I had, but expressed curiosity about how the book had relevance to my circumstance. The pastor asked me what my wife's love language was. I told him and he said, "So there you go." I responded with "huh?" so he clarified. "Operate from your wife's love language to communicate with your staff. Treat them based upon your wife's love language because it will become natural for you to sustain." Best advice ever. My wife proved to be a mix of "words of affirmation" and "acts of service" and both cost nothing more than being genuine.

Establishing how to communicate to build relationships was key in my steps to build momentum toward the changes the school needed. I saw that the trajectory of where we would end up rested heavily upon how much staffers trusted me—and upon their willingness to follow because they understood my heart and I theirs.

And then, there was the other possibility.

Maybe the right people weren't in the room. Maybe those I needed to discuss and share and think through tough decisions were not a part of the team. I needed not to assume that those who were in leadership needed to remain there. Considering this possibility, I offered to meet with every leader to discuss whether they wished to continue in their current leadership role. It was not until after the meeting that I realized my way of making the offer hadn't been received as I'd intended. While I intended to provide an option for those who would prefer to take a backseat, I stepped onto a landmine by using the word "inherited" as a lead-in to the meeting request. I have now placed the term "inherited" among the lexicon of "educationese" curse words. I spent the following day sending an email explaining that I meant no malice but had spoken as a matter of fact. At the time I considered the reaction to be silly. It quickly proved to be a lesson in learning not to be dismissive of how my words can make others feel. Even though it wasn't my intention I didn't make them feel valued. I wasn't clear or kind. As leaders, we can quickly lose our subordinates if we fail to read the room or refuse to address something we've said. I also learned about the leaders in the room. My words could arrest them emotionally, but no matter what I believed we accomplished in that meeting, it had been erased by an unintended offense, and without a word that gave me the indication that I offended them.

Having the right people in the room isn't simply a matter of having people who agree with me. It was a matter of the stakes that I understood we were playing for. The work that needed to be done required courage and innovation. At the bare minimum, I needed people close to the work who cared enough about what we do to tell the truth, so that all of us can make the best decisions. Even when the truth didn't feel good, it was necessary if we were to grow. In time, the right people were in the room and they were willing to have courageous conversations. One person at a time. To get there it took redefining the expectations of the position. For some, this was not something that he or she could live up to. With others, it came down to coaching, to help then work through leadership gaps that prevented them from becoming the leaders I needed them to be. We were going to share in the heavy lifting but first we had to be clear about where we were going, who was going to carry what and how fast it was going to take to get there.

## WHOSE TEAM ARE YOU ON?

In my pursuit to figure out how to lead a varied group of people, I stumbled upon a seminar that changed my outlook on the staff. Prior to becoming the principal, I worked for principals who often analyzed their staff based upon a model of productivity. I vividly remember listing teachers and placing them in certain quadrants that reflected the intersection of productivity and maintenance, whether high or low for each characteristic. While we worked through the exercise to discuss where staff fell, the process seemed to make a lot of sense. Watching Anthony Muhammed's Transforming School Culture seminar, I saw that he focused more on the psychology of the educator, which evokes behaviors that affect teachers' approach to their roles. Muhammed highlighted the traits of four types of people (Believers, Tweeners, Fundamentalists and Survivors), and described what these types did in an organization and how to handle each. My mind was blown. I never considered the psychology before—which is silly because I often say that we are in the heart business. The work that we do is driven by the mindset of the educator. How children are shaped has everything to do with how educators feel about themselves in the work.

This was crystallized for me because I understood how to engage, and I also knew what I needed to do to identify the right people for the work ahead of us. By Muhammad's definition, I needed more Believers than Fundamentalists. I needed to find ways to get Tweeners connected to the business of school and the activities of our students. This newly found information begged more questions. How do I shape teacher mindset? What do I do to change the culture of the adults to breed the workplace attitude that will encourage them to step up to get it done? My willingness to address these questions changed everything for me.

Everything I envisioned for the school was grounded in my understanding of how I should communicate, and how I should guide, direct and develop the talents of staff and students. We had to begin by looking inward. Those who were still at the school during the changes had to commit to wanting to be there, in truth and in form. I was motivated by the stakes. Education was what changed my life. It provided an opportunity to break a cycle and carry the torch for my family to a different level. My son has not known me without having a terminal degree. My son has not known me to not be in a leadership position. My daughter watched me attend school and has lived through the elevation in my career. She was present at my dissertation, when I was called Dr. Broadhead for the first time. I am in the position to create a structure that can catapult students into their own. I can create an environment that fosters and encourages opportunity through a rich environment. We can build confidence by showing children things they did not know existed. I am in charge of this. These are the stakes. I know firsthand the positive impact of education. I am indebted. With these stakes, I did not need anyone who just wanted summers off. I needed everyone to develop the mindset and the energy to accomplish what was necessary.

To solidify the process of identifying the right personnel, I had to share my vision. This was the only time I created an idea in a vacuum. I stepped from my office hoisting the stone tablets that carried my vision over my head. It was still just a notion. It was not the plan to get us there. The goal was down the road but it was attainable, and a reasonable thing to strive and fight for—every year. I moved forward with this idea in isolation because I wanted the staff to understand that I wanted more than just "doing school." I wanted better than the old status quo, so I had to articulate this early. I also wanted them to know that I had a short-term plan and a long-term plan. Showing them a five-year plan was my way of telling those Fundamentalist naysayers that I was planning to stay, and see the plan through. More importantly, with all that the staff had gone through, they needed consistency and direction. The clearer I was, the better it was for me to take a hard look to see who wasn't going to stick around for all this vision talk, and who accepted the challenge of where I wanted the school to go.

From the revelation of the plan to the execution of it, I took it upon myself to observe more and listen to what the staff was telling me, verbally and through their actions. In faculty meetings and leadership meetings, we could be in agreement but I wanted to see how it translated to daily practices, and the conversations among the staff.

## EXORCISING LIMITING BELIEFS

No matter what I believed could exist at the school, if the staff didn't believe it was possible, then the vision was dead on arrival. The experiences of some staffers led them to limit their thinking, and to believe that "these kids" couldn't, didn't deserve, or would refuse to improve. Cultivate that attitude and the foregone conclusion becomes a self-fulfilling prophecy. Sadly, I found staffers who existed in pockets of negativity, working feverishly to maintain a mindset that I no longer wanted to thrive at the school. I no longer wanted staff members to feel comfortable speaking negatively about the school or the job or any aspect of what we were doing. I wanted solutions. I wanted behavior to change. I wanted the unwilling "survivor mentality" to leave. I noticed adult behavior that suggested, passively, that some staffers were not on the same page as I. Other teachers were more blunt: I heard, far too often, negative judgments of children who had made poor choices. One male educator told me, with audacious candor, "You *know* this kid is a piece of shit!" Because we weren't yet wearing COVID masks, I used every one of my facial muscles to remain expressionless. All I could muster in the moment was, "I don't know that, but I think you need to step away from this." When a female teacher shared her frustration about a student who refused to stand for the Pledge, she said, "It's like he acts so entitled." I was struck by the remark because the problem plainly didn't lie as much with the student as with the way the teacher elected to share her displeasure.

Some educators just didn't like the students. The students were tolerated. A clear "tell" for me was how the teacher responded to student misbehavior. Teachers who reprimanded in a mean-spirited way that didn't leave the student with any dignity nevertheless expected that the student show them respect. Well, in the aftermath of a visceral negative interaction, that was unlikely. In some instances, the manner in which a teacher talked to the student took the form of a personal attack, which made it very hard for the teacher—or me—to defend. When addressing a lack of professionalism, I stressed the importance of remembering that these children are *children*; and I posed a hypothetical: How would you react if your child had been spoken to by a teacher in the same way you just spoke to your student?

Outside of not really liking the students, there was another staff issue that also stemmed from trauma: the need to win the battle of control. Teachers wanted to make it very clear to the child that *they* were the authority, and that consequences would be doled out based upon their word. This battle derived from some teachers' perception (which was their reality) that the administration could not control student behavior. These teachers responded to negative behavior in ways that mirrored what they thought the administration should have been doing all along. Clinging to the notion that nothing instructive was going to happen to the student after being turned over to admin, teachers developed an "overkill" response to behavior issues, because it gave them control of the immediate exchange *and* provided a moment in which to deliver their displeasure, and to sleep well at night, whether or not an admin ever spoke to the student afterward.

There were instances in which staff members took credit for their instructional practices only when it benefited them, while explaining away poor student performance by saying, "These kids don't" or "can't. I took note when suggestions in leadership meetings centered on student behavior, and policy changes that might make it easier for the teacher to cite the policy to protect a callous response to off-task behavior.

I saw enough under-par adult behavior to recognize that more staff members than I would have liked to believe wore educators' cloaks while carrying on like resentful volunteers at a homeless shelter. They cared about the recognition for being there more than they cared about the work that might make a difference in the lives of the people they served. Correcting behavior came from a place of offense rather than redirection.

Sometimes when we came close to addressing a problem, staff

reflex was to reject the reflective thought that might help solve the issue. That scared me because the reaction willfully ignored things that principals and staff can control. In those moments of rejection, I could foresee the collapse of my vision. By no means was this the majority, but enough pockets of this mindset existed that, if left unchecked, would prevent us from becoming the school I believed we could be. In front of me I saw what others did not see, and some *refused* to see. I saw great children who needed adults to help them achieve their potential. My vision wasn't about me. Yet, there was no ownership from staff for their role in reshaping the realities of the children they saw every day. I witnessed the beginning of how a school becomes a failing institution. I knew that resistant staffers didn't realize the danger of the road they were headed down, so I had to make it clear in a faculty meeting how their actions affect where we end up. The common culprits were listed:

- Closed-door leadership
- Relying on state assessments alone to determine our achievement
- Focusing solely on remediation

It was in this meeting that I explained the characteristics of a failing school. After that, I asked the staff to complete a survey telling me why we might share the same fate. The responses revealed harsh perspectives that I had to accept as what was in their hearts. What stood out the most was the statement, "The kids act like animals," accompanied by direct shots at me and my guilt-wielding Blackness.

Thanks.

I received many other direct attacks that were surprising, off-putting and disheartening. I quickly learned that an anonymous survey is better for some teachers than therapy. He or she can dump pain and negativity with more bitterness than a jilted lover. Only a few told me that we weren't going to be a failing school, and they were not going to allow it to happen. This is what I'd wanted to hear from *all* the staff. When I didn't, the necessity of the changes that needed to be made were crystallized for me. We had some ways to go. I needed to figure out how to cut through and sustain a new mindset that would allow the vision to become a reality.

It took a lot for me to refrain from sharing the responses of bigotry and animus. I desperately wanted to hold up the vitriol, to show them that nasty sentiments would not allow us to move forward collectively. Fortunately, I realized that my initial desire to share the negativity was rooted in my hurt. It was about revenge and making those anonymous voices get a taste of fear, because I would be sure to make everyone uncomfortable enough to see who started turning red first. But I wasn't here for that, and anyway, it certainly wouldn't change their hearts or the circumstance. It would be a cop-out for me to choose anger over responsible authority. Before the work I wanted to do could be carried out, I'd have to devote constructive energy to the challenge of changing attitudes.

We needed to be of one accord. Before I could assure families of what we were providing their children, we had to confront the worst part of who we were. I couldn't fail to deal with our demons. It took courageous conversations. We had to face the root of issues.

As mentioned earlier, I was working in a professional culture where everyone talked *around* issues, because it was easier and more polite to do so. I had some choices to make. I could join them in the dance of polite avoidance, and cover myself by hinting that people like them (though certainly *not* them, per se) might kinda sorta have some responsibility to help address a school's challenges, whereas if it *were* them—which it isn't, because I'm not accusing or insinuating—so . . .

Nah.

- ✓ I have a concern. I would like for us to talk about…
- ✓ Please help me to understand…
- ✓ This is what I saw. This is what I heard. Was there more that I missed that would better clarify?
- ✓ We are the adults in the equation, so let's talk about how we can get different outcomes.
- ✓ We are the only ones that chose to be here. The kids *have* to come or their parents go to jail.
- ✓ You made a choice that you should live up to. This is what you said you wanted to do in your interview. How have things changed?
- ✓ Let's not decide on something you can't live up to. I want a positive shift.

Speaking to the problem was a big finger-wag in their direction. No one had figured that addressing the root was what needed to happen, and that to do so would benefit everyone. To do anything else was a disservice. I knew that there were faculty members who saw the negativity and felt that it was not their place to say anything. They wanted certain behaviors and conversation to stop. By confronting those who needed the conversation, I presented a clear line for what was expected, and let selected individuals know that I saw them working against my expectations. There was no crowd to hide behind., no room for the individual to seek comfort in anonymity. We were eye to eye, and I shared everything that I noticed about their behavior if it had a direct impact on our trajectory. Their discomfort was something I could live with because I knew that, in time, they'd no longer use the building as a sanctuary for their negativity. No more commiserating within these walls. Some made it easy for me by continuing their bad decisions, I helped them pack their things so they could seek new homes elsewhere. I welcomed the idea of poor staffers departing as much as good ones who stayed.

In all of this I learned how to separate my emotions from the big picture. It was not going to be about how I felt about the individual but about how that individual's actions influenced our children. I had to invest in knowing how to communicate directly without the perception of malice. I didn't want those who were doing right by their students to be misled to believe that they too had to worry about their jobs. Again, this was not about might and fear. This was about addressing what was not right and making those who were not good for our kids to choose to be better or move on.

The reality of these experiences wasn't entirely unexpected, but it was unsettling. It revealed a new wrinkle in the work that I had to embrace to ensure that children were getting our best. My APs and I had to think through ways to invest in our staff, to help them focus on the reasons why they chose the profession. We vowed not to be an obstacle for our staff. The work was hard enough. The intention was truly about all of us being better.

I had to acknowledge and accept that my position has power, and that every word I used carried weight. Whether I liked it or not, there was always a caveat. I had to embrace it. By doing so, I had to put more emphasis on allowing time for things to improve, and to develop natural-seeming contact points that the staff could understand as I intended. I had to allow the consistency of my actions and words play the part it needed to without a rush to a resolution.

The greatest equalizer was time. Over several years, I utilized the time to demonstrate my heart and consistently show that I cared about the role of the teacher; I did whatever I could to empower them. For professional learning, I looked to the staff. For new positions, I did the same. Decisions were made as a collective, and when decisions needed to be made from my office I did so, but respected their right to know what my thinking had been. I apologized publicly and one-on-one when necessary. Accountability was important. I was okay with the idea that I'd make decisions that wouldn't suit everyone. I wasn't okay with those who weren't okay as professionals, and chose to speak their mind outside of the forums provided to share their concerns. I cared for my staff and did whatever I could to show them that my words matched my actions. This is how I utilized my time. Prior to getting to a place of where teachers felt comfortable coming to me directly (even if they had a concern with my leadership or a decision I made), I experienced some key moments that made me reflect, and dictated adjustments that allowed me to be a better communicator as the principal.

Two milestones gave me validation that what I had set out to accomplish internally was finally gaining the right traction. The first was in alignment with the work. I knew I finally made the headway I set out to make when the leadership began communicating with their respective departments using "we" when discussing the work that was ahead of us, and stopped saying, "He wants..." This small difference showed me that they understood that ownership wasn't mine alone. They had a stake, and carried the burden, as well. For this, I couldn't be more pleased. Prior to this shift, my follow-up conversations with individuals on the leadership team felt as if the staffers had been assigned a report, in which they'd have to review what I'd said to them. They thought they had figured out their roles as leaders, and that I'd be satisfied if they merely parroted back to me what we had discussed. I told them countless times that that was not who I needed them to be. I could tell the staff myself if it was just a matter of restating what they heard me say. To finally see them internalize the work and handle their part could not have made me happier. They were embracing the idea that I trusted them to lead.

The second milestone was more powerful to me because it was a shift in the culture. I am not talking about the overt culture that is promoted to get everyone on the same page. I mean the culture of beliefs that manifests outside of the structured meetings, and can negatively affect what happens at the school. These are often frustrations about policies, procedures, evaluations or decisions made by administration that are discussed in parking lots or workrooms. Unspoken grievances that breed contempt and decisions to operate independently rather than what the group has agreed upon.

Two interactions stand out to me. The first situation is one I never saw coming. A teacher, Ms. Mary, approached me, worry etched on her face, to share that a colleague spoke ill of another colleague by using racial slurs. Not only did she tell me this, there were two others who came forward and shared their concern as well. What touched me most is that Ms. Mary said that when she heard her colleagues' comments, she could not believe that that person could say such a thing and work at the school. Grief-stricken, she repeated the statement, "What about our kids?"

Ms. Mary measuredly stated that she thought of me immediately, and could not hold in what she'd heard. Although appreciative that she felt compelled to tell me, I couldn't let the association of how hearing a teacher call another teacher a "nigger bitch" correlate directly to me. I had to get clarity.

Ms. Mary explained that she remembered the story I told them during a faculty meeting about being racially profiled by the police. She emphasized how struck she was by how I described I was treated. She was bothered by how wrong it was. She was bothered by how wrong her colleague was. Ms. Mary connected the hate that lived in those words to words she heard before growing up—words she chose never to use. She understood the power in the word and connected the hate not only toward her teammate but to our Black children and to her Black boss. Ms. Mary saw how we were all connected by this hate, and could not understand how a white woman who could use that word, love our children, and have respect for her boss. She learned that these two things could not be true.

During my first few years at the school, I felt a need for tough conversation about race empathy, and the general ignorance of the experiences of Black people. Police shootings of unarmed Black men and women were becoming the headlines more frequently. In the grand scheme of life, these incidents reminded me of my insignificance. I wanted something to change but felt powerless to do anything. My staff was more diverse. Unfortunately, some staff members held opinions of the circumstances surrounding the murders that were offensive and callous—to me. I couldn't grasp how an educator who taught at a public school didn't possess empathy. When a school counselor retweeted a post that suggested that the victim deserved to die, I couldn't just walk the halls, hold meetings and conduct business as usual. I could easily be another headline as a Black man slain for resisting arrest. Yet, somehow, the educators I led had the luxury of being able to distance themselves. I couldn't allow that. We needed to talk. We needed a moment for us to see each other.

> Unapologetically Me: *We all have bias. There is something that we each carry in us that prejudges someone for something. Yes, we all do. You may not want to admit it but here is your test. You claim that you do not have a bias toward an obese person—until that heavy guy or woman starts walking toward your row on the airplane. I am sure*

*you now understand what I mean. Even in that situation our bias is not really hurting anyone because you have no power to stop that person from sitting anywhere on that plane. But here, you are the pilot. You have power. You may claim that you have noooo bias but you do. I will prove it. Think about the student that gives you a hard time. Picture him or her right now. I bet you can see that student. You know that student's first, last and middle name, don't you? Now picture next year. It's the first day of school. The marker is still fresh on your whiteboard when you find out that the student you can't stand has a little brother or sister in your class. How do you feel about that student now? Will you give that new student a clean slate? Yes? No? Maybe? You might until the day that child shows any signs of behavior that reminds you of their sibling. That student is going to have to work ten times harder and repeat that behavior every day just to change your mind. As the teacher with power, how you feel based upon your bias can alter a child's educational experience. None of you are any different from what is happening in the world. You are not above human error. However, when you work at a public school you must be receptive and open to the possibilities that exists from all walks of life. We don't get to be close-minded about our families who have different religious practices, beliefs or ideas. We must reserve judgment.*

It was during this faculty meeting that I shared a childhood experience and several other encounters I had with the police based upon an assumption that I could be breaking the law. I shared the lifelong fear of the police I developed as a result of those negative interactions. The staff needed to know that, despite what *they* know about me, the police do not. If I fit a description, I can easily share the same fate of those brutally beaten or murdered. I can lose my life over a policeman's bias.

The conversation opened up the floor for others to share their stories, and we all got a glimpse into the fears of our colleagues. The meeting became more than what I ever intended, and it was better than what my soul needed. It was clear to me that what I had shared was not lost on the offending teacher or her colleagues.

Other staffers who were privy to hear firsthand from the mouth of the staff bigot met with me to express professional disappointment, and great concern that a person who felt that way was working with our children.

The reality of what their colleague said was bigger than simply dismissing negativity or worrying about someone other than the children we served. Every staffer knew that this was not right, and none were willing to sit with this behavior from a colleague who served Black and Brown children while holding contempt in her heart for Black people. I could not have been more proud of their courage to come forward.

The second situation will make you scratch your head and wonder why it became a shining moment for me. A teacher came into my office and closed my door behind her. I watched as she stood in front of the closed door and just started in: "Yesterday in that parent conference you made me mad..."

I sat and listened to all that she had to share about why she was offended, and everything she did after the meeting other than flatten my tires. I let her finish and then thanked her for coming to me. I couldn't have been happier. I was not surprised that she was upset with me. I'd seen during the meeting that she was upset, and I could even put my finger on the moment when it happened. I'd become accustomed to her usual approach to dealing with her professional anger. Unwilling to come to me directly, she would share with other teachers her own version of what had happened; it was through the other teachers that the angry reaction would finally filter its way to me. But on that day, the teacher's behavior changed. She stabbed me in the front and I loved every bit of it. I now knew that she understood me. She respectfully vented without having to worry about getting fired, or suffering other retaliation. What was gained in that moment was honesty. No cloak of a survey. She was hurt. She wanted me to know. She felt she could be heard. She dumped in front of the person who hurt her. My position mattered but it did not matter. And when it was all done, we were in a better place.

This is what I worked for. Courageous conversations were no longer coming just from my office. They were happening among colleagues in team meetings and behind closed doors one-on-one. Ownership began to take shape. No one person was going to derail our progress. The importance of communicating and holding each accountable became the order of the day. The awareness that we all had a part to play in the story we were writing was evident. Collaboration. Ownership. High expectations. What I had hoped for and envisioned was in front of me.

# THE PERCEPTION

Prior to my arrival, the school's reputation was not positive. A lot of what was being said arose more from fear and ignorance than from truth. What was being accepted as the status quo for this school was overlooked at other schools in the system. The school had its problems but their existence was amplified, while other schools in the area were not defined by their problems. Consequently, this had an impact on parents' decision to allow their children to attend. Having recognized this as a hurdle, I made a point to address the misperception. I needed to stop the bleeding. I needed to build trust in the community, to help parents understand that I too wanted the best for their children, and was not interested in lowering standards. Given the task ahead of me, I did what I thought made the most sense. I wanted to make myself available and provide as many opportunities as I could to change minds. Misperception stung because it is lazy and dismissive. Misperception comes with a consequence for Black people, so I am sensitive to it, especially when businesses or schools are judged on nothing more consequential than how many Black people are present. To extend the point further, I hate that there is even quicker rush to judgment if a Black person represents ownership or is "in charge." Assumptions are made that are not positive. I don't subscribe to any of it, so I automatically operate from the standpoint that this school will not be less than or not good enough because it is a majority-minority institution. I carried the weight of transforming that mindset. However, I didn't care how everyone felt about the school. I cared about how our parents felt and how the children felt. I learned very early that those who are focused on being against you will never be *for you*, so why work to change their hearts? My only plan was to bring the community a sense of pride in their school and let them know that the institution provided everything the kids needed. If the parents of my students didn't like the school, didn't like the opportunities it provided or felt we offered fewer opportunities than elsewhere, it was important to me to investigate and determine how to ensure that level of equity.

During job interviews, candidates have asked me what I like most about the school. I appreciate the question. I often answer that the school has a level of diversity that is a gift and a curse. The gift is that diversity doesn't exist only in complexion. It exists in culture, economics, academic support and enrichment opportunities. It exists in the gifts and talents of the children, as well, so the opportunity for students to get a snapshot of what America looks like as it was intended is possible here. The curse is that the diversity begets a diversity of needs. There are so many nuances to master. There is no group too small to be ignored. Attention must be paid to all. Because of such a wide range, the demands and needs of parents are parallel.

One of the challenges faced by every principal is parent engagement. Either there is too much, too little, or too much about the wrong things and too little about the right things. As a new principal trying to establish myself, it was hard for me to differentiate who should have my ear, and which issues really had to be solved and which were ones to tuck away for later. I asked questions and listened. I tried my best to filter the manner of delivery of the concern and pay attention to the concern itself. According to what parents told me, the school did very little for those students who accomplished good grades. The parents felt that the school did not celebrate the achievements. The students should be encouraged and acknowledged through honor rolls and accolades. We fell short. It was brought to my attention that certain opportunities didn't exist in comparison to neighboring schools. There were schools that had a Science Technology Engineering and Math (STEM) program and other special programs for their students and we didn't. It was brought to my attention that the teachers were racist and the administration just wanted to lock children up. Parents who had my ear were vocal, and pulled no punches in telling me how awful the school was. I entertained every conversation with an open mind because I thought that nothing they were complaining about had to do with me...yet. However, it all had *everything* to do with me. The ritual of meeting parents and hearing complaints became my starting point, a cheat sheet I used to determine what needed to change, after I absorbed the great variety of concerns expressed by individual families.

In as much as parents shared their concerns, I also felt an

overwhelming amount of support from the community. When the school hosted its open house I had a long line of parents waiting shake my hand and introduce their children to me. Each parent welcomed me and thanked me for being there. Many expressed hope and excitement that I was there. One parent asked that I bring the school back to what it once was. Others told me that they will not let me fail. I received many encouraging words that I will never forget. I also felt some level of pressure to deliver. The weight came with the genuine expectation that things would change for the better because I was now the principal. It was a tremendous feeling, and I accepted the challenge wholeheartedly.

Parents' areas of concern showed me that what I thought was pretty clear about school was only clear to me and about 100 of my good friends—who all happen to be educators. The crux of parents' issues boiled down to miscommunication, misconception and misunderstanding. I can understand why. Consider how schools, for the most part, interact with their school communities: parents are left to sift through meetings and paperwork and policies for simple answers. But parent frustration, ignorance or confusion was in some ways our responsibility. As educators, we make assumptions about what parents should know, and are unforgiving in our disappointment in them for not knowing. But the system itself has its share of blame.

Based upon what I learned about the community, I sought to change what we could control. Since there was a trust issue, I had to figure out what conjured the feeling. Drawing from basic school practices, I thought of how often or how little parents are given an opportunity to become engaged at school. I had to ask myself about context for parent events and what is expected of parents in those settings. It dawned on me that parents were not given many touch points for a two-way experience with admin or staff unless the issue was unwanted behavior. I considered the student who doesn't get in trouble, ever. Will the parent hear from the school for any reason? Why do we as a school engage with parents? What is the tone of our conversation? What if the parent just doesn't know? What is the history of that parent with schools? How much different can we be from what the parent has experienced in other schools?

There is a key factor in American culture that is overlooked. It is the culture of education, and the people who make it run. Sometimes, educators forget to be their own best advocates. We forget that the majority of us always wanted to be in education. For various reasons, we made decisions that married us to learning. For most, the experience of being students brought positive feelings of success. And from being a successful student, we made the transition to being a teacher or counselor or support staff. We capitalized on our strengths and our comfort with knowledge, utilizing our individual pockets of success to create the foundational support we needed to move forward.

Since entering education in Pre-K or kindergarten, we never left. Let that sink in. *We never left*. Everything about what school is and its nuances are parts of a teacher's DNA. What educators consider to be "common sense" and "clear" is not *common* or *clear* to the average parent, who ran as far away from school as they could to begin their careers. Some suffered through school to get to do what they truly wanted. For most people, re-entry to public school is directly tied to having children. Their only reference point to what happens at school or what the experience might be comes from what they experienced during childhood. Consequently, there is a huge gap of understanding that cannot be ignored.

Whether we like it or not, time must be taken to ensure, explain, repeat and assist. We often take it for granted that a great proportion of parents comes back to the school system with reservations rooted in long-ago school-related trauma. Even if the majority of parent experiences were positive, it's the one negative experience that parents not want their children to face. We must be mindful of triggers that can cause educator-parent interactions to derail.

It is because of these triggers that parents send emails at 2:30 a.m.—IN ALL CAPS. Triggers also bring parents to the front office as soon as the doors open, demanding to speak to the principal. These reactions are fueled by their own childhood traumas combined with the stories they were told by their children the night before. Emotions can run high and push parents into full protection mode. Blinded by the reminiscence of pain, they show up to make sure that the school that may have failed them or someone they know doesn't fail again.

During my first year as principal, I didn't understand why parents behaved this way. I had many interactions with parents earlier, when I was an assistant principal, and heard a range of responses during my calls to parents. Quite often they were upset with me, and with the school as a whole, based upon disciplinary measures, or our explanations of what their kids had been involved in. There were also those who were very supportive, despite being disappointed by the choices their child made. More often than not, there was a parent who showed up demanding to see an administrator immediately. My colleagues and I always assisted, but each of us had a moment of pause. The parent's conviction that his or her concern should be attended to immediately was a stinging level of audacity. It flew in our faces because of an assumption that administrators did nothing but wait for problems, and that there could be no good reason to delay handling the parent's emergency.

Discipline was a task, but it wasn't the definition of our roles and responsibilities

I carried that frustration into the principalship. Parental concerns, that in every case (as I saw it) had nothing to do with me directly were not going to make me stop handling whatever I was in the middle of before they showed up. Their concerns would have to be addressed outside of my presence; I'd follow up later. I held on to this mindset until I realized that the parents who came in to talk to me almost always left upset *with me*. My reaction to their concern shifted the original concern, which may have had nothing to do with me, to a complaint to the district office about me. The district office would call me and then I'd follow up with the parent. In almost every case the issue was resolved and the parents were be fine. I finally came to the conclusion that there was no good reason beyond ego that this roundabout way of handling complaints should be the routine of my interaction with parents who "just show up."

I learned that the mindset of a parent who walks in the door upset before breakfast is in a very sensitive state. Parents have to alter their day to do that, and if I didn't see them, I'd be ignoring their sacrifice. Last but most important is this: As a man, a father, and a husband, the only thing that could pull me out of character and cause me to willingly send myself to jail would be to defend my wife or my children. If in my heart of hearts, I believe that an adult or another child at the school is mistreating my child and I need to do something about it, I too would show up to the school immediately to get the problem solved. As a principal, I have other things to consider, but I do completely understand—and am sympathetic to—the upset of parents.

I could not ignore the raw and real feelings of a parent who finds out that his or her child is hurt or defenseless. Parents' reaction is to protect, to show their children that they have their backs, and are willing to do whatever is necessary to protect them. When parents fail at that, they are diminished in their own eyes, and in the eyes of their children. I could no longer ignore what motivates the upset parent who sits in my office on the phone, a foot tapping uncontrollably. I now chose to understand. I was okay with walking into the situation without all the answers. Parents needed me to listen to whatever the scenario was, and follow through. This approach did wonders in helping to establish trust and credibility with parents. I did not want them to feel that I was the only one that could help, but I did want them to know that I cared about their children and would do my best to make difficult situations better.

This understanding forced me to think about the part our current practices play in reinforcing a lack of trust and negative perceptions. Systemically, where can we start, and when we do, what will be the outcome?

The work that was ahead of us started in the classroom but was pervasive. What are the policies that may promote a negative interaction? From the front office to the custodial office, what are we communicating? I found myself focused on branding and marketing. I reviewed the school website to see what we are telling the world about the school. I searched social media, as well. I streamlined communication and emphasized that there should be only one voice that speaks for the school. To challenge practices and policies that were not districtwide was essential. We had to question the expectations surrounding parent communication, and reflect upon the reasons why staff communicates with parents at all, and how. With what frequency? By what means?

After evaluating what we already had in place and revisiting our underlying intentions, I made the decision to provide more opportunities for parents to engage with the school. The parent liaison was going to be essential in identifying where parents needed support, and to create programs to speak to those who needed it. I held more parent meetings throughout the year and requested feedback. Our conversations, as well as the information that was being shared during stakeholders' meetings, were done to ensure clarity and transparency. The focus was on sharing what our plans were, and how we needed parent support to make the plan a reality for the students' benefit. We hosted more events that were centered on building community outside of sporting events. We celebrated culture, academics and talent. We invited parents in to have breakfast with their children, and interacted as a school with those who attended. We hosted school tours and invited parents into classrooms. In time, our parents felt confident in the direction of the school and understood what was important to us. We were no longer prisoners of perceptions based in hearsay and generalizations.

In the world of social media, parents were now willing to defend the school if a parent decided to use that outlet to air out an issue they were having. To see a parent tell another parent how to communicate with the school, and to reinforce the idea that administration works to solve problems, was a breath of fresh air. The work that we had put in was paying off. Those with a gripe were encouraged to take the proper steps to get their problems solved. When a new family inquired via social media about the school, other parents provided honest and objective criticisms. Although parent remarks were positive and glowing, I was more focused on the fact that they were honest and not mean-spirited. We were not perfect. However, it was always my focus to be viewed with respect and given a fair critique. Our demographics alone should not give anyone license to bash the school.

Outside of what was put in place structurally to welcome, inform and support parents, the most important aspect of gaining the trust and credibility of parents are the experiences their children have in the classroom. How our children are made to feel by the adults in the building is paramount in the short-and long term.

When talking with teachers about the experiences our children have in the classroom, I asked them to reflect on how they build relationships, and to consider the impact of building community in their classrooms. How do you show children that you see them? Genuinely *see* them. Student attitude affects achievement. If our kids feel that the teacher doesn't like them, they reject every aspect of what that teacher represents, including the assignments and learning process. Some students are not strong enough to focus on their goals if they believe they are not liked by staff. By being mindful of this point, I reinforced the reality of the teacher's power in the eyes of children. Every word, every moment we choose to spend praising, supporting or admonishing is tallied. The same goes for kids' parents. The parent knows which teacher contacts them only to discuss negative behavior, and those who contact them for the good, bad and just to inform. What the educator does to create credibility and trust is more important than what I do as the leader. I have fewer contact points than the teacher. Ninety-six percent of my meetings with parents are based upon what happens in the classroom.

With this in mind, I asked the staff to think about the types of meetings *they* have with parents. I asked them to consider which of the parent meetings could have been avoided by doing some work on the front end? Parent conferences are often initiated because of reactions to practices that were not put in place by the teacher. If teachers communicate equitably, the parents give the benefit of the doubt, rather than engage negatively and accusingly. Are there still instances where parents make unreasonable demands? Yup! However, those parents are outliers and not the norm. It takes more care, not more work, to provide parents with what they need to know to ensure their child is in good hands at school.

Perspective is everything. Embracing this wholeheartedly was important for me to learn as I grew into the role. Listening provided the window to perspective. I may not agree with another point of view, but an understanding of perspective helped me grasp *why* a parent, student, or staff member made a decision or responded a certain way. Without being open to understand the "whys" of a behavior, I would not have had the insight necessary to make informed decisions. The closer I have been able to get to an understanding the psychology behind the school community, the easier it has been for me to examine the proper solution.

I made no overall sacrifices of one group over another. The bottom line is the success of our children. To get there, all of us must understand the assignment. Each of us owns our part to give our children the best chance for success, while at the same time understanding where our part starts and ends. Each year the fight was to remind everyone what their responsibilities are while we supported each other, instead of working against each other. We translated the rules of school for parents. We reinforced the policies and expectations to the children. Each of us became a model and an exemplar for others on the staff. We noted small wins and adjusted to failure. I created and delivered my sermons to each group to maintain the right focus. I tried to crystallize the action plan. My job was not to make staff members feel good. The stakes are too high. I had to be sure to preserve what made the school what it had been since its inception, and find ways to create something new for all to embrace as the future of what the school was going to be.

# BECOMING ENOUGH

I have to start with the demons.

I am a dreamer but I am also a believer. My inclination to want more for myself was born out of being frustrated by what I believe I deserved. It was also born out of a feeling of being less than anything my mind considered to be greater. Between **deserving** and *less than* there lived **fear**. I feared the idea of being insignificant. To have lived a life of total inconsequence. To not have contributed or be held in any regard. To be thought of with indifference. Yet, a lot of me believed that I possessed nothing that could change the course of my trajectory. I could foresee a plain straight line. Nothing special presented itself. There was always someone somewhere who did ...than me.

Later, when faced with moments of acknowledgment, I could not accept the moment. *No spotlight, please.* We did it. *They did so much more.* No... thank *you*. Me? *I could not be "better than" because there's nothing to see here.* Look that way. *This is nothing.* Someone is out there working harder. *Don't you celebrate.* Humble yourself and get back to work. *Nobody cares.*

And because this internal battle existed I never believed that I was good enough.

Then Doubt, with his big head, would show up in the midst of everything. Moving my stuff. Questioning all my bright ideas. Asking me to answer questions I never thought of but have now begun to worry me. Looking at me all stupid. Doubt has a look. Doubt made me compare myself to other teachers, writers, APs, speakers, and leaders. It changed how I looked at myself. It created room for me to believe criticism. When a student, in anger, said, "You can't teach no way!" I agreed. Especially after he failed to insult me in proper English. When others were acknowledged for what they were doing in the classroom, I wondered why I wasn't. If, as an assistant principal, I wasn't asked my opinion or perspective in the decision-making process, I wondered why my words had no weight. I believed seniority would allow my voice to be heard.

When reality set in and Doubt took over, I sat in my car with tears streaming down my face, trying to figure out how to matter. When the reality of becoming the principal was spoiled by the feeling in the back of my mind that it came to be only because they needed a Black man to lead Black and Brown children, Doubt whispered in my ear. Doubt questioned my success in the eyes of higher ups who believed that the school's success couldn't be attained with my leadership. Doubt made me question whether my earrings caused my intelligence and experience to leak out my head; they definitely defined me in the eyes of those who needed to see me as less than. Doubt caused others to wonder if I can speak to *all* people. Doubt made me wonder if the people I led would see me differently if I were not the one leading them. Doubt made me wonder if I was effective. It affected me deeply. I wanted to walk away from education, pack my shit and unpack the story of how the system sucks to an audience of those who lost hope in *all* systems.

Be wary. Doubt is as contagious as a yawn.

Yes. The moments of vulnerability are real. This line of work is not easy. It never was.

Yet, when I decided to become an educator I believed I was going to make a difference anyway. I never thought it was going to be easy. I didn't fully anticipate the degree by which it was difficult, and where obstacles might arise, but I never thought that making a difference was a cake walk. I resolved that my choice to be accomplished was stronger than any people or conventions that might become obstacles along the way.

The children mattered. Despite the frustration I felt, it all came back to them, no matter where I served or what my role was. I made adjustments. I created programs. I stayed late. I built relationships. I hired and trained people who love children and want them to succeed. I created a new philosophy. I made those who did not like children feel uncomfortable. I recommended that those who did not care for children find something else to do. I added opportunity and created new avenues for children to learn and to grow. I connected. I supported. I made a point to see those who were often overlooked because, just like them, I felt the same way. I...I...I me me me...unapologetically me, and I did that in every space no matter what title I held. I did it without fear and sometimes without permission. With each choice I made, the hope was that whatever I provided would make an impact that reverberated beyond me. To create a thing that could exist by itself and yield *good*, exponentially, was always my intention. To my surprise. No fanfare needed. It all mattered.

I always did.

Not just because of any one thing. I mattered at every moment, and I mattered most when I believed I mattered least. I was who I needed to be for that time for those children and for those staff members, and for that parent, to become what I need to be during every encounter. In each phase of my life, when I sat in confusion and worked through it, I was becoming. Fueled by the willingness to offer more to those who I believed needed a better shot at life than I, fear and doubt eventually no longer bullied me. There now stood confidence. Accepting myself gave me strength. Loving myself gave me freedom.

I will not allow another person's opinion of me to overrule the opinion I have of myself. I refuse to allow someone's ignorance to justify how I should see myself. I will not change who I am for someone else's comfort.

I no longer look for others to make it okay for me to be me.

I no longer ask the question: "Where are the Black men in this profession who are...so I can...like them?"

I will be the one I am looking for.

I will look no further than the mirror and the vision I create for myself to determine my trajectory.

I am more than a suit, a degree, articulation, earrings, or physique.

I am a complex human being who makes choices rooted in the complexity of years of life experience. Who I am does not disappear behind any title I earn. I've been me longer.

It is okay to be alone in my thoughts. After all, they are my thoughts.

And *this* is where I leave *you*.

# ABOUT THE AUTHOR

DR. MARCUS L. BROADHEAD's career has spanned two states, four degrees, four high schools, three middle schools, roughly 500 colleagues, and over 50,000 students served over twenty years. He has had the privilege of working with students from seventh grade through college before going into educational administration.

As a New York native and Georgia resident, Dr. Broadhead entered the field of education as an English teacher under the premise of wanting to do more than just teach Shakespeare. Having recognized early in his career that he could inspire students not to defer their dreams, he began creating opportunities for students after school. Building mentorship programs and serving as a sponsor for extracurricular activities confirmed the need to support students beyond his role of teacher. He credits much of what he has accomplished as an educator to his time in the classroom, and focuses on seeking connections to empower as the basis for his approach to leadership.

For Dr. Broadhead, being an educator holds the weight of the responsibility to truly educate and be a resource to all with whom he comes in contact. He currently serves as a principal, and supports educators through talks on parent engagement, empowering others, and purpose driven leadership. He also volunteers his time to speak to youth on perseverance, making positive choices, and goal setting.

Dr. Broadhead earned his Bachelor's degree in English and Master's in Education at Hofstra University in NY. He furthered his education by adding Ed. Leadership to his Master's degree through The University of West GA, and received his Specialist and Doctoral degrees in Educational leadership from Argosy University.

His accomplishments are not defined by his accolades or measured by the number of programs he has created, supported or led, but by the individuals he has positively influenced. Being part of the solution is on his daily to-do list, with an emphasis on moving a community forward through those who have the power to change lives.

However, he never loses sight of his utmost priority and legacy: his wife, Lisa, and his children, Taylor and Aiden.

Learn more at www.marcusbroadhead.com.

Made in United States
North Haven, CT
04 February 2022